The Beginning of My Beginning

Freedom: From Religious Rituals to Intimacy with God

By Latonya Sterling

The Beginning of My Beginning
Freedom: From Religious Rituals to Intimacy with God
By Latonya Sterling

Scripture quotations, unless otherwise noted, are taken from the **[NIV, ESV, KJV, New King James Version®]**. Used by permission. All rights reserved.

ISBN: 979-8-218-73679-8

First Edition – August 2025

Cover design generated ChatGPT, adapted from original artwork by Marcel Sterling

Published by Latonya LSimmons Sterling

Contact: latonyasterling@gmail.com

Printed in the United States of America

"It is for freedom that Christ has set us free. Stand firm, then, and do not let yourselves be burdened again by a yoke of slavery." — Galatians 5:1 (NIV)

Father,

Thank You for Your help, by Your Spirit in writing this book. I pray that whoever reads these words will be encouraged in their hearts. May this work never be used as a tool to criticize churches or leaders, but rather as a guide—drawing each reader to recognize their personal responsibility to draw near to You.

I pray they will learn to seek You, commune with You, and grow in their relationship with You, so they are no longer bound by the traditions of man. May they come to see the value of fellowshipping with other believers and the joy of giving.

If any reader has been wounded by the church, I ask that You help them surrender that pain to You. Heal their hearts. Bind up their wounds and mend what has been broken. Let godly sorrow lead them to true repentance and let genuine growth take root in their lives.

Help them become who You have called them to be and live in the liberty of grace You've given through Christ Jesus. I thank You in advance for revealing Yourself to them—helping them know You more deeply, understand who they are in You, and walk as servants of righteousness, free from the bondage of sin and manmade traditions.

In Jesus' name, Amen.

Table of Contents

Introduction

"From Performance to Intimate Communion"

I spent many years as a believer living a performance-based life. I thought that if I could just "do enough," "be enough," or check all the right religious boxes, I would finally feel close to Father—or at least acceptable to Him. But no matter how hard I tried, I was failing miserably. Behind the scenes of my devotion was a heart weighed down by striving, shame, and silent exhaustion. I didn't truly understand Father's love. I didn't grasp the significance of Holy Spirit living inside of me. I had no real sense of my identity in Christ or the power I had been given to live free from sin's grip. I was trying to please a Father I barely knew, following rules I didn't question, shaped more by the traditions of man than the truth of Scripture.

I had learned how to behave, but not how to abide. I knew the motions of rituals, but not the depth of relationship. I was full of expectations, but empty of intimacy. Outwardly, I appeared to be a "good Christian," yet inwardly, I felt disconnected trying to honor the Father without truly knowing Him or the Holy Spirit within me. Everything began to change when I finally began to study the Bible for myself—not out of obligation, but out of desperation. Slowly, the Word became more than ink on a page. It came alive. It revealed the heart of the Father, exposed the lies I had believed, and invited me into truth. It drew me—not to performance—but to intimacy.

When I originally wrote this book, my subtitle was *Freedom from Religion to Intimacy with God.* But after spending some time with God, I realized I was misusing the word *religion.* The word originally means a system of faith and worship, but over time it has often become associated with a rigid structure of man-made rules and traditions. I want to honor the true meaning of the word rather than misuse it. So, I chose to use the phrase *religious rituals* instead.

5

I trapped myself in religious routines—following practices that looked spiritual but weren't grounded in true understanding. I was going through motions based on things I had heard, personal assumptions, and my own limited understanding of Scripture. I was reading the Word, but I wasn't studying it for myself. That's where I went wrong. I neglected my relationship with God, elevating rituals over real intimacy, mistaking activity for obedience.

Intimacy with God is far more important than a system that sounds like God but is entangled in human effort, expectation, and appearance—something that can mask the simplicity and freedom found in a true relationship with Him.

This book is for every born-again believer who feels stuck in the cycle of spiritual striving. It's for those who long to know the Father but feel distant from Him—those weighed down by traditions and religious rituals, unclear about their identity, or unsure how to experience the power and intimacy promised in Scripture. This isn't a book about church hurt because I've always served with great people, nor is it written to blame any pastor or church community for where I once lacked understanding. I take full responsibility for not doing my due diligence in studying the Word for myself. This message is not meant to condemn—it's meant to call you into deeper communion with the Father who loves you and gave His Son for you. We were never meant to live chained to man-made traditions or empty rituals. We were created to walk in relationship—with the Father, through the Son Yeshua HaMashiach (Jesus Christ), by the Spirit—and that relationship comes alive through the Word.

As you read this book, my prayer is simple: that you'll be drawn back to the Bible, and through it, to the heart of Father. I pray that you'll see His love, discover your identity, and begin walking in the freedom and fullness of a life that honors Him not just outwardly, but from the inside out. Remember, victory comes through trusting God and believing biblical truths—not performing religious works. Let's begin—not with performance, but with intimate communion.

Chapter 1: My Story

My household didn't go to church regularly when I was a kid. Dad never went to church. Mom sporadically took us places far and in between. But Mom never stopped us when others invited us. When I was around 13 years old in junior high school (that's what it was called then), one invitation changed my life. Petrina Whitehead invited my sister and me to a little storefront church, that used to sit on Lafayette Boulevard in Norfolk, Virginia, called The Way of the Cross.

That Sunday morning was anything but ordinary. The sanctuary was filled entirely with kids. At the front stood a young man—possibly a youth pastor—teaching with colored chalk and an easel. As he taught about Jesus dying on the cross, he drew an image of Golgotha, showing Jesus and the two thieves beside Him. You could hear a pin drop. Every child was captivated. That moment marked the first time I ever heard the story of Jesus, the Savior of the world.

From this sanctuary, we later went to smaller classes based on our age. Petrina and I were in the same class even though she was older than me. There was this sweet-faced woman who taught the class. I don't remember anything she taught accept she kept talking about this Jesus. After class, Petrina and I stayed behind, because after hearing about Jesus, we wanted to be saved. The sweet teacher led us in a prayer to accept Jesus Christ as our Savior. After we finished, she asked, "Do you feel anything?" I didn't—but I lied and said I did. That was my first lie, told moments after I'd confessed Jesus as Lord. That moment marked the beginning of my wrong thinking. She didn't teach me that salvation was confirmed by a feeling, but in that moment, I misunderstood her question and thought that if I didn't feel something, it meant I wasn't truly saved." When I think about it today, she was probably excited for us and wondered if we were excited as well.

Disillusionment and Detour

I believed I was saved—but I did not fully understand what salvation really meant. I thought salvation made me perfect instantly because now Jesus lived in me. That illusion shattered the day I argued with my aunt and said something mean. My mom overheard and said words that would define the next eleven years of my life. She said, "I thought you were saved. Saved people don't talk like that." Mom didn't mean any harm. She simply said what she believed. Saved people aren't supposed to say mean things to other people. But, being a teenager with no understanding, a seed was mistakenly planted that the reality of my salvation was marked solely by my behavior. Those words crushed me. I felt like a failure, disqualified from serving God. I went to my room, got on my knees, and prayed: "God, I don't know how to be saved. I'm not perfect. So, the next time I get saved, please lead me to a church where they will teach me how to live right. But God, I can't be saved right now." For the next eleven years, I believed I was no longer saved. Yet, no matter how much I tried to live life on my terms, there was always something—someone—tugging at my heart. I later realized that it was Holy Spirit in me, the seal of a salvation I thought I had lost.

The World Couldn't Satisfy

By nineteen, I was clubbing regularly. By twenty-one, I had a VIP pass to a nightclub called David's. I was a student at Norfolk State University and living life my way. Then I met Duane, a charming but inconsistent friend who disappeared and reappeared often. Eventually, I learned he had been living a double life. But, his final return was different. Duane had met Jesus while at a rehab facility in North Carolina—and now he wouldn't stop talking about Him. It irritated me, and I dismissed Duane as a fake. "He'd be a heathen again," I thought in my mind. In the meantime, I was still living my life … at least trying to. But, Holy Spirit in me was like a background noise that I couldn't identify, yet I couldn't escape. So, all the fun I thought I was having always ended with me having feelings of guilt or shame. I could not understand why I always felt bad. There was also Duane who wouldn't give up on his foolish friend—me.

Back to the Father

Here it was my birthday weekend. I was about to turn 24. I celebrated at Septembers, a high-energy dance club that used to sit on Greenwich Road. The night was everything a club night should be— live crowd, music, dancing, and attention. After dancing the night away celebrating, I called it a night. As I walked to my car, something strange happened. I started talking out loud, saying, "I've found another place to hang." I was excited about a new spot to hang out at on the weekend. Suddenly, a wave came over me. I stopped, looked back at the building, and said, "No devil. I'm never coming back here again." That was the last time I went clubbing.

The next day, Sunday, October 3, 1993, Duane called. We talked about God, and for once, I didn't argue. Then he asked a question that stopped me cold: "Well, Miss Simmons, since you know these things, why aren't you saved?" I had no answer. While he kept talking, I was in a silent mental battle. Everything he would say to me I was combating it in my thoughts. He was ministering on all six cylinders. Car people will understand what that means. I literally told myself in my head that I couldn't say yes. Then he said, "Don't let the enemy make you think you can't say yes." How did he know my thoughts? It was like God gave Him access to my thoughts. The dam broke. I cried uncontrollably. Duane prayed with me. He thought he was leading someone to Christ for the first time. But in truth, Father was calling His backslidden daughter home—honoring the prayer I prayed as a confused little girl who thought she had failed Him forever.

The Community That Raised Me

Duane had joined a church community led by an incredible teacher. To my surprise, a woman named Valarie Rose—who had been gently ministering to me at work—was also a member of that community. I had even watched their pastor on TV and once said to myself, "If I ever get saved again, this is the church I will go to." He was such a practical teacher who taught in a way that a child could understand. So, when Father drew me back, that ministry was where I went.

When I first attended, I knew I had a rebellious streak. I asked God to send a strong woman of God to help me grow. Although I had become a born-again believer at 13, I lived the next eleven years as a backslider because I had no guidance to help me grow. A backslider is a born-again believer consistently living as one who is not born again. Through this community of believers I went through follow-up, new converts class, and new members class. It was after the new member's class that my prayer for a mentor was answered. Enter Mom Dotson—a spiritual mother who pursued me with love and became my mentor. Later, Dad Dotson was added to my heart and became a father figure in my life, gently and consistently helping shape my walk with Father. I learned to read the Bible, to pray, to fast, to serve in ministry, to lead with character, and to train others to lead. It was a time of incredible transformation. However, as years had gone by, I realized something was missing.

Even though I was surrounded by good people and mostly sound doctrine, something felt off. I couldn't explain it at first, but deep inside, I knew though I loved the people, something was missing. I was faithful, but I wasn't free. I was productive, but I wasn't at peace. Somewhere along the way, I had learned how to perform for God instead of simply being with Him. The rules, the expectations, and the silent pressure to always be "on" began to weigh me down. I started to feel like I was living in a box—one built not by God, but by how I interpreted the things I was taught. So, I cried out again, "Father, I love You, but there has to be more!" Even though I prayed, it took some time for me to see what "the more" was.

The Missing Piece

While at this church community I met a wonderful single father, Marlon Sterling, who I eventually married. Three years into marriage we had our first child together. By the time our first son was a toddler, I had stepped back from full-time work. My days were quieter, filled with long stretches of downtime while Marcel napped or played. I was still active in ministry, but something inside of me was still unsettled. There was a hunger I couldn't name, and a discontent I couldn't shake. I had everything I thought a godly life was supposed to include—salvation, a wonderful husband and kids, church family, spiritual leadership and ministry. But, in quiet moments something was off. It wasn't a crisis of faith. It was a cry of a heart that knew there was more. One day, while flipping through the channels at home, I stumbled upon a familiar preacher, Creflo Dollar. I almost changed the channel—until something he said froze me. "God loves you unconditionally—not because of what you do, but because of who He is." For the first time in years, I felt gripped by a message of God's love. It wasn't a message of rules or striving for perfection. It was just love—pure, unconditional love. From that day on, I watched Creflo Dollar every chance I could. I took notes like I was in school. Truth after truth began chipping away at the walls my wrong thinking created around my heart. I realized that I didn't know God for myself. I was born again, but I had become so caught up in spiritual activity that I hadn't developed spiritual intimacy. That lack of intimacy kept me bound in some areas of my life. So, much of what I did brought no true fulfillment. My brain couldn't process why I was so discontent when I was serving God ... so I thought.

A Journey into Freedom

Because I was watching a religious channel to see Creflo Dollar, I came across Joseph Prince. Despite his accent, I was captivated by his teaching. His book Destined to Reign and later The Power of Right Believing shattered the remnants of performance-based Christianity in me. Through his teaching, I learned that righteousness is not something I earn, it's something given to me from God that I needed to receive. Freedom is not a goal, it's a gift. I also learned the difference between the old and new covenants. Moreover, I learned that the way I thought contributed to how I lived.

Through watching Creflo Dollar, I also discovered Andrew Wommack, who was a guest teacher. His quiet, steady teaching of grace and identity in Christ took me even deeper. I devoured his books—at least twenty of them. Each one dismantled another lie I had believed about God, myself, and what it meant to be "good enough." Reading his books with God's Word helped me so much.

The more I studied the Word, learned about Holy Spirit, read books and listened to sound teaching, the chains of religious bondage and sinful behaviors started to fall. I could see clearly that I had been saved but living bound. I was born again, but boxed in. I had spent years trying to please God through serving in church—all the while missing the simple truth that He already loved me fully, deeply, and completely—apart from my performance. I was no longer afraid of making mistakes. I stopped striving to be perfect. I began enjoying growth, not just serving Him. I discovered peace that didn't come from doing—but from believing. It didn't happen overnight. It took years to unlearn the performance mindset and become rooted and grounded in Father's love. I'm still on that journey today—a journey of increasing freedom and intimate relationship with Father, as I am being transformed, not by rules, but by grace. Can I take you on a journey of freedom through the grace of God?

A Prayer to Truly Know God and Walk in His Truth

Father,

I want to know You—not just know about You. I don't want to be bound by man-made rules. While I understand that not all traditions or boundaries are wrong, I want what matters to You to matter most to me. Teach me to recognize the difference between what is truly from You and what is merely human preference.

I'm not rejecting structure, but I don't want anything—no rule, no opinion, no expectation—to hinder my relationship with You. I open my heart to Your truth. If there's anything I've believed, accepted, or followed that has kept me from truly knowing You, please reveal it to me. Help me walk in the freedom that comes from Your Spirit, not the pressure of manmade traditions.

According to John 6:44, it was You who drew me to Jesus. And now, as I draw near to You, I thank You—based on James 4:8—that You are drawing near to me. May our intimacy grow deeper, and may I walk daily in the freedom that flows from truly knowing You.

In Jesus' name, Amen.

Latonya Sterling

Chapter 2: Still Becoming:
The Journey Continues

Grace Isn't the End—It's the Beginning

Discovering grace wasn't the final chapter in my walk with Father—it was a brand-new beginning. Everything I thought I knew had flipped on its head. For the first time in my life, I wasn't chasing God's approval—I was living from it. I didn't have to strive to be enough. In Christ, I already was. But the journey didn't end with freedom. It just changed direction. Instead of performing, I began to pursue. Instead of faking perfection, I started embracing progress. I stopped trying to become someone else's version of a born-again believer—and started becoming who Father originally designed me to be. This was so liberating.

Relationship Over Routine

There were days I missed the routine. The predictability of manmade rules can feel safe. But I had tasted something sweeter—intimate relationship. In this new place, I learned that God didn't want my checklist. He wanted me. For years I had believed that my relationship with God was only as good as my performance. If I did the works, my relationship with Father was intact. If I slacked from works, I didn't have relationship with God, and I had to do something to get it back. But, Father showed me something different.

Relationship – A State of Being, Not an Action

Many of us have been taught that having a relationship with God is something we do – that it is about how often we go to church, how many chapters of the Bible we read daily, how many hours we

15

spend in prayer, or how faithfully we serve in ministry. While these practices are important for spiritual growth and intimacy with God, they do not create the relationship itself.

Relationship is not a verb. It is not an action word. Relationship is a *state of being*. It describes a connection or a bond between people. By definition, relationship means "the way in which two or more people or things are connected, or the state of being connected" (Oxford English Dictionary). It is about *who* you are connected to, not *what* you do to maintain that connection. The moment we come to Christ and accept Him as our Lord and Savior, we are connected to God. Jesus Himself is the bridge that connects us to the Father; therefore, our relationship with God is established through Him alone.

A simple example is marriage. A husband and wife are related through marriage. Even if they separate for a time and do not live together, they are still married – their relationship status has not changed unless they officially divorce. Likewise, our relationship with God is established through Jesus Christ and cannot be undone by mere distance, struggle, or weakness on our part.

In the Old Testament, God spoke to His people, Israel, saying, "Turn, O backsliding children, saith the LORD; for I am married unto you…" Jeremiah 3:14 (KJV). Even when Israel turned away and walked in rebellion, God still called them His own. He declared that He was married to them – meaning their relationship remained, despite their unfaithfulness. This wasn't an approval from God of their sin. It demonstrated his faithfulness to the covenant He made.

This is how it is for us under a better covenant. I reiterate, we are related to God as His children, not because of our works but because of our faith in Jesus Christ. Works such as prayer, reading His Word, worship, and serving are not what establish our relationship – they are what helps us to grow and creates intimacy with Father.

Because the words relationship and intimacy are often used interchangeably and sometimes misapplied, many believers have come to believe that if they don't consistently do the things that foster intimacy with God, their entire relationship with Him is lost. But, what's interesting is that neither of these terms—relationship or intimacy—are used in Scripture the way we often use them today. The Bible simply and clearly shows us that we are connected to God through Jesus Christ. If we are saved by grace through faith—not by works—then it makes no sense to believe that we could lose our salvation simply because our works fall short. Some people quote the verse, "faith without works is dead" (James 2:26), but often misunderstand its meaning. It's not a call to perform works in order to prove our faith. Rather, it's a reminder that genuine faith naturally produces actions not from striving or obligation, but from trusting God. To trust means to rely upon. Learning this was a game changer for me.

What the Father has shown me through His Word is that I am related to Him through Christ alone. My salvation is secure because it is rooted in what Jesus has done, not in what I do. However, my consistent time in the Word and communion with Him deepen my intimacy with the Father and help me grow within that relationship. A lack of intimacy didn't erase my relationship with God—it just kept me spiritually immature and more vulnerable to the influences of my flesh, the world, and the enemy. That is definitely not a place to stay. Heaven forbid a person stays in this place so long that they actually denounce Jesus Christ as Lord. Nevertheless, intimacy is about growth, not qualification.

Always remember: You are God's child because you believe in what Christ did for you on the Cross. Your connection to Him is your spiritual identity. Your good works grow you within the relationship, but they do not create the relationship. It is Christ alone who makes you a child of God. Moreover, as you learn to trust Father you will grow, and your behavior and works will reflect your true identity.

Becoming Is a Lifelong Journey

I've been saved for decades now, and I'm still becoming. I'm still learning; still shedding old ways of thinking; still receiving fresh revelations of Father's goodness; still being healed; and still growing deeper in my identity as a daughter—not a servant trying to earn favor.

In my journey, I discovered that before I could really know who I was, I had to know Father. This was more than knowing that He is an invisible God who lives in the spirit realm of Heaven and sent His Son Jesus Christ. This is a Father who has a nature and a character. And, because I am made in His image, I needed to know what that image looked like.

Reflection and Responses

Ask yourself:

- In what ways have I treated grace as a finish line instead of the starting point of my journey with God?
- Have I been approaching my relationship with God more like a routine or a real connection?
- What does "becoming" look like for me in this current season?

A Prayer of Thanks for Relationship, Not Performance

Father,

Thank You that I don't have to earn Your love or approval. Thank You for the gift of relationship with You through Jesus—not based on my performance but fully grounded in Your grace. I am so grateful to be called Yours.

But Lord, I don't want to settle for just being in relationship with You—I want intimacy. I want to know You deeply, to grow closer to Your heart, and to walk in step with Your Spirit. Help me to hunger to know You more, not out of duty or routine, but out of genuine desire. When I open my Bible, help me to discover more of who You are. When I pray, I want real conversation—not obligation—where my heart opens to Yours.

Teach me to slow down, to listen, and to seek You with my whole heart. As I draw near to You into deeper communion, thank You for drawing near to me according to James 4:8. Let every moment of worship, study, and prayer become a place where intimacy grows and trust is strengthened. Thank You for inviting me near—not because I'm worthy, but because You are loving.

Help me rest in the truth of Your grace, and out of that rest, grow into deeper fellowship with You every day.

In Jesus' name, Amen.

Latonya Sterling

Chapter 3: Father – Who Are You?

One of the most sobering things I've learned is that the day I got saved, I knew almost nothing about God—only that He is God and that He has a Son named Jesus who died for me. That lack of understanding became clear in how quickly I gave up as a believer when I thought I had to be perfect for Him. I never believed that all my problems would disappear once I got saved. What truly disillusioned me was the false expectation that I was supposed to become perfect immediately. No one ever told me that—I simply assumed it. I had been told that Jesus would come to live in me, and I figured that if the Perfect One was living inside me, I would somehow become perfect too. What I didn't understand at the time is that perfection isn't instant. It's a lifelong journey—a process called sanctification. And for that process to even begin, I had to begin to get to know the Father—not just know about Him.

As I continue to share my journey from religious rituals to intimacy, I'm reminded again and again that everything starts with knowing the Father. I don't mean having surface-level knowledge or being able to quote Scriptures—I mean truly knowing Him as the One who created us, who loves us, and who longs for intimacy with us.

Throughout Scripture, God reveals Himself as Father. Jesus often referred to Him this way, and when He taught the disciples to pray, He didn't say "My Father," but "Our Father"—inviting all of us into that same deep, personal fellowship with a holy and limitless God. (Matthew 6:9, NKJV)

So, who is God? The answer is beautifully layered, but it begins with this truth: God is love (1 John 4:8). That means everything He does flow from love—not from obligation, anger, or distance. But love is just the starting point. Scripture also tells us that God is holy (Isaiah 6:3), completely set apart and pure in all His ways. He is just (Deuteronomy 32:4), always doing what is right, and at the same time,

He is merciful and compassionate (Lamentations 3:22–23), extending grace we could never earn. He is our Creator (Genesis 1:1), the One who formed us intentionally and knows us completely. He is our Father (Matthew 6:9)—not distant or detached, but kind, patient, a loving disciplinarian and deeply personal. He is faithful (2 Timothy 2:13), meaning we can trust Him fully—He keeps His promises, even when we fall short. He is all-knowing (Psalm 147:5), all-powerful (Jeremiah 32:17), and ever-present (Psalm 139:7–10). And yet, with all that majesty, He invites us to draw near. God is not some force or an abstract idea—He is a Person, and He wants to be known.

I don't claim to know everything about Father. But what I do know is that He is more than amazing—He is beyond description. Every new thing I learn about Him leaves me in awe. This isn't an exhaustive writing about who God is. But the most important thing that I want to share in this book is what changed my life. God is your Father and He loves you because He is Love!

God is Love

If you've been in church as long as I have, you've probably heard teachings on the different types of love. We've been taught about *agape* love—often described in the church as God's unconditional love. This term agape was used in Koine Greek text of the New Testament. But to the Greeks, *agape* simply meant a general love or goodwill toward all people while the church coined it as *unconditional love*. Then there's *eros* love, understood as romantic love between spouses; *storge*, the love of family; and *philia*, the love between friends.

All of these are Greek concepts of love. The Greeks, in many ways, were a morally corrupt society, both in practice and philosophy. It's worth asking how did the church come to adopt their definitions of love as the standard?

The truth is, the Bible doesn't teach us Greek love—it teaches us that God is love. 1 John 4:8 (NKJV) says, "He who does not love does not know God, for *God is love.*" (Italics added)

In Scripture, we don't just get definitions—we see love revealed through the very nature and character of God. 1 Corinthians 13:4–8 (NKJV) says, "Love suffers long and is kind; love does not envy; love does not parade itself, is not puffed up; does not behave rudely, does not seek its own, is not provoked, thinks no evil; does not rejoice in iniquity, but rejoices in the truth; bears all things, believes all things, hopes all things, endures all things. Love never fails …" Read that passage again, but replace the word "love" with "God." It hits completely different, doesn't it? This truth is life-changing. Because God is love, everything He does flows from who He is—not from who I am. That means His love for me isn't based on my actions, my performance, or even my faithfulness. I have heard songs with the line, *"I don't know why God loves me."* I do know why—because He is love. I certainly can't earn it, and I can't lose that love. It's not about what I do or don't do. And honestly, I can't even put into words what that realization does to my heart.

When some people say they love someone, they're often just expressing temporary emotions based on how they "feel" at the moment. It is also too often based on the other person's behavior toward them. But biblical love is demonstrated to others despite their behavior. Romans 5:8 (NKJV) reminds us, "… God demonstrates His own love toward us, in that while we were still sinners, Christ died for us." None of us living today were born when God demonstrated His love toward us. Moreover, He demonstrated it "before" we were saved. Catch that! The fact that God loved me before I ever became His child—before I ever turned to Him—is overwhelming. Especially now, as His daughter, that truth is even more powerful.

When believers don't understand that God is love, it becomes hard to receive His love. Many of us were raised with the idea that love must be earned—and we unconsciously project that mindset onto

23

God. That's exactly what I did for so long. Knowing who God is builds on our foundation of Jesus Christ. Growing in God's love produces lasting fruit. The more clearly we see Him, the more we begin to understand who we are—and how deeply we are loved. This became by motivation to press into knowing my Father.

Reflection and Response

Ask yourself:
- Who do I believe God is beyond what I've been taught or heard?
- How does knowing God as love affect my desire to draw near to Him?
- What attributes of God do I find hardest to understand or accept right now?

Prayer of Thankfulness to Know Father

Father God,

Thank You for allowing me to know You intimately—not just as a ruler, but as my loving Father. Thank You that Your love is freely given and that I don't have to earn it, because You are love itself. I praise You for creating me, guiding my steps, and caring for me each day. Thank You for teaching me through Your Spirit and lovingly disciplining me—not out of anger, but out of a heart that desires my growth. I am grateful to walk with You as my Father and Friend.

In Jesus' name, Amen.

Chapter 4: Identity:
In My Father's Image

In Genesis 1:26-27, God says, "Let Us make man in Our image, according to Our likeness..." and then proceeds to create humanity. What does it really mean that we are made in the image of God? It's a phrase many of us have heard in church, but it often leaves us wondering—especially since God is Spirit. Clearly, this doesn't mean we physically resemble Him. So, what does it mean? Being made in God's image means we reflect aspects of His nature, His character, and His authority. Unlike any other part of creation, humans were uniquely designed to mirror who God is.

First, we reflect God's nature. We've been given a spiritual capacity—the ability to know God, to commune with Him, and to respond to Him in worship. We possess a moral nature that allows us to discern right from wrong, to love, and to choose. We are rational beings, created with the ability to think, plan, reason, and create—just as God is intelligent and creative. We also experience a wide range of emotions such as joy, sorrow, anger, and compassion, which mirror the emotional depth of our Creator.

Second, being made in His image means we were created to represent His authority on earth. Genesis 1:28 speaks of dominion— God entrusted us with stewardship over creation. That doesn't mean domination or abuse of the earth, but rather a sacred responsibility to care for what He has made. We are His representatives, called to reflect His justice, mercy, and righteousness in how we live and how we treat others.

Third, our design reveals that we were created for relationship. God is relational—Father, Son, and Holy Spirit existing in perfect unity—and we, too, are wired for relationship. We are meant to live in deep connection with God, with others, and with ourselves. Our identity, value, and purpose are all rooted in that relational design.

While sin distorted the image of God in us, it didn't destroy it. Even in our fallen state, every person still carries inherent value because of that divine imprint. And through Christ, that image is being restored. As 2 Corinthians 3:18 tells us, we are being transformed into the same image from glory to glory by His Spirit as we look into His Word. As we grow within the relationship with Father, we begin to reflect Him more clearly—not physically, but in character, in holiness, in love, and in purpose. Being made in God's image means far more than simply existing. It means we are called to reflect who He is, to represent His heart and authority, and to live in continual, growing relationship with Him. That is both a beautiful identity and a lifelong journey.

Once I began to see myself as being made in His image, I started to discover who I truly was. I began shedding parts of my character that didn't reflect Him. I stopped using phrases like, "This is just who I am," to justify long held attitudes or behaviors that didn't align with His nature. There are still things in me that God is working out, but the more I come to know Him, the easier it is to recognize what doesn't belong.

Knowing God has freed me from the pressure of becoming who others think I should be. As I grow in relationship with Him, I've gained confidence in who He's called me to be. I no longer rely on compliments or opinions to define my worth. I'm not chasing approval through relationships, appearances, or performance. I've been set free to simply be who He created me to be—without pretending, striving, or hiding, and my value and worth are found solely in Christ. It's not based on how I look, what I've accomplished, or what others think of me. I am valuable because God created me. I am loved because He is love. That truth alone silences every lie that ever told me I wasn't enough.

For too long, I believed my worth had to be earned—through performance, attention, or relationships. But God's love isn't something we achieve; it's something we receive. My worth was established before I ever did anything right—or wrong. Like David, from the moment Father formed me in the womb (Psalm 139:13–16), He called me valuable. The cross is proof of how much I matter to Him—not because I'm perfect, but because He is perfect, and He chose to redeem me.

In Christ, I am accepted (Ephesians 1:6), and I am chosen (John 15:16). My identity isn't anchored in the world's ever-changing standards; it's rooted in the unchanging truth of God's Word. I no longer live trying to earn love—I live from the confidence of already being loved. That's where my worth begins and ends: in Him. And the beautiful part is this: anything in me that still needs changing, I trust my loving Father to reveal it—gently and faithfully—by His Spirit who lives within me.

Not Still A Sinner Save By Grace: A New Creation In Christ

For a long time, I saw myself as a struggling Christian. I believed in Jesus, but I still saw myself through the lens of failure, shame, and sin. I thought I was just a sinner trying hard to be righteous—never realizing that Father had already redefined me the moment I was born again.

Many believers today walk through life saved, yet still spiritually insecure. They don't know who they are in Christ. They accept Jesus as Savior but continue to carry the same mindset they had before: broken, unworthy, and bound. This is not how we were meant to live. When we become born again, we receive far more than forgiveness—we receive a new identity. But until we know who we are, we'll keep living like who we were.

"Therefore, if anyone is in Christ, he is a new creation. The old has passed away; behold, the new has come." — 2 Corinthians 5:17 (ESV)

You're not a cleaned-up version of your old self—you're a completely new creation. Your spirit was made alive by the power of Father. The "old you" died with Christ, and the "new you" was raised with Him. But if we don't renew our minds with truth, we'll still think, speak, and act like our old selves. That's why the Word of God is essential—it teaches us who we really are.

Traditional teachings might tell you, "You're just a sinner saved by grace," but that's not what the Word says about someone in Christ. The Bible says you're a child of God (John 1:12), the righteousness of God (2 Corinthians 5:21), a co-heir with Christ (Romans 8:17), and seated in heavenly places (Ephesians 2:6). Moreover, when Paul writes that "while we were yet sinners, Christ died for us" (Romans 5:8), he reveals both God's love and the transformation that takes place in Christ. Before salvation, sin was our identity—we were born into Adam's disobedience and therefore made sinners. But through Jesus' obedience, we are no longer defined by sin; we are made righteous (Romans 5:19). This means that in Christ, "sinner" is no longer who I am, even if I sometimes stumble. My identity has shifted. I am now called righteous, a new creation, a saint, not because of my works but because of Christ's finished work. Sin may still occur in my behavior, but righteousness is now my nature, my standing before God, and my true identity.

Understanding who we are in Christ is essential to how we see ourselves and how we live in the world around us. When we know that our identity has shifted from sinner to righteous through Jesus, we begin to see ourselves through God's eyes instead of through shame or failure. This identity not only allows us to receive His love toward us more freely, but it also moves us to reciprocate that love through obedience. Living from this truth shapes the way we respond to struggles, relationships, and even our own mistakes, empowering us to walk in confidence, freedom, and intimacy with God.

Adopted Into Sonship

"The Spirit you received does not make you slaves, so that you live in fear again; rather, the Spirit you received brought about your adoption to sonship. And by him we cry, 'Abba, Father." Romans 8:15 (NIV)

Father didn't just save you—He adopted you. You are now His child, not a spiritual orphan trying to earn approval. This changes everything about how you relate to Him. When you understand your identity as a son or daughter, you stop trying to earn what's already yours. You stop praying like a beggar and start living like someone with access. You stop performing and start abiding.

What's Next

Now that we've began to explore who God is and what it means to find our identity in Him, the next question becomes: how do we truly *get to know* this God who created us, loves us, and calls us His own? One of the primary ways we come to know Him is through His Word—the Bible. The Bible isn't a book of tall tales or religious rules; it's God's living, breathing message to us. Through Scripture, we see His character, hear His voice, and receive His guidance. It's in those pages that we begin to understand not only who He is, but how He moves, speaks, and relates to His children. If we want to grow in relationship with God, it is absolutely advantageous to spend time in His Word.

Reflection and Response

Ask yourself:

- Am I living out of who I am in Christ, or out of who I used to be?
- Do I approach Father like a child or a performer?
- Am I letting Scripture define me, or am I still shaped by people and past pain?

Prayer of Thanks for True Identity in Christ

"Father,

Thank You for making me a new creation in Christ. Help me to fully understand and believe who You say I am. Strip away every false identity and replace it with Your truth. Help me to live a life that flows from my identity—not insecurity. Teach me to walk as Your child, full of confidence, peace, and freedom.

In Jesus' name, Amen."

Chapter 5: The Living Word: Studying for Yourself

For many believers, the Bible is either treated like a book of rules or a religious relic—quoted, respected, even feared—but not truly known or encountered. Yet everything we need for life and godliness is found within it. Our freedom, identity, and intimacy with Father becomes more realized through the Word.

I used to think reading the Bible was just part of the Christian routine—something you do to be "a good believer." But that mindset turned the Bible into a checklist. I didn't realize that neglecting to actually study the Word meant neglecting one of the sources of Father's voice in my life. It wasn't until I made a personal decision to study the Bible for myself, not just rely on sermons, devotionals, or church traditions, that my spiritual life began to shift.

The Word Is Alive and Active

"For the word of God is living and powerful, and sharper than any two-edged sword, piercing even to the division of soul and spirit, and of joints and marrow, and is a discerner of the thoughts and intents of the heart." — Hebrews 4:12 NKJV

Father's Word isn't stale or outdated—it's living. That means it still breathes, still speaks, still penetrates and transforms. It reaches into the places that traditions and rituals can't touch: the deep motives of our heart, the places where we hide, the lies we didn't know we believed.

The Word doesn't just inform us—it forms us. It teaches, corrects, encourages, confronts, and reveals. It's one of the means of how we hear from Father, how we learn His nature and how we test truth from error. Without the Word, we are vulnerable to deception—even if we're surrounded by religious language.

31

All Scripture Is God-Breathed

"All Scripture is God-breathed and is useful for teaching, rebuking, correcting and training in righteousness, so that the servant of Father may be thoroughly equipped for every good work." — 2 Timothy 3:16–17

Some people believe that "God-breathed" means everything written in the Bible has God's stamp of approval. But that's a misunderstanding. The Bible being God-breathed means that God inspired men to record what is written—for our instruction, correction, and growth. That doesn't mean every action or decision described in Scripture reflects God's character or His will. Think of it this way: God breathed life into us, but that doesn't mean He endorses every choice we make. If that were the case, we'd have to believe God approved of David taking Bathsheba, or countless other sinful actions recorded throughout the Bible. Instead, Scripture gives us a full and honest account of humanity—our failures, our need for redemption, and the faithfulness of a God who remains holy and just through it all.

Father didn't leave us in the dark—He gave us His Word so we could know Him, walk with Him, and be equipped to live lives that truly honor Him. Some of us unknowingly trade the voice of Father for the opinions of man. We follow secondhand revelation—what a pastor, parent, or friend said about God—instead of going directly to the source. They may be right in what they teach or say. But Father wants to meet us personally, not just corporately.

There was a time in my journey when I assumed everything in the Bible applied to me in the same way. However, as I continued to grow in relationship with Father and studied the Word more deeply, I began to understand the importance of scriptural context. I realized that while not every passage was written directly to me, all of it was written for my learning (Romans 15:4). That shift didn't diminish the value of Scripture—it deepened it. I may not experience every situation described in the Word firsthand, but I can still draw wisdom from it.

And often, God uses that insight to equip me to walk alongside others facing those very things.

For a long time, the Bible felt more like a rule book than a relationship guide. I didn't yet understand the difference between the Old and New Covenants, and because of that, I found myself influenced by a mixture of teachings that blurred the lines between law and grace. No one intentionally misled me—many of the voices I learned from were sincere and genuinely loved God. But like me, they were also growing in their understanding. Looking back, I realize I had unknowingly embraced a kind of *cross-contaminated doctrine*—well-meaning, but sometimes confusing—which often left me feeling condemned rather than free. I don't mean abolishing the moral law of the Old Testament and the prophets, because God's law is good. I'm talking about performance-based living rather than being led by Holy Spirit. As the Holy Spirit began to illuminate the Word more clearly, I discovered that Scripture isn't meant to burden me but to lead me into deeper relationship with God through Christ.

Thank God for teachers like Creflo Dollar, Joseph Prince, and Andrew Wommack during the time I felt lost. I'm not saying their teachings were flawless—but there was enough truth in what they shared to point me in the right direction. Their messages stirred a hunger in me to seek God for myself and to study His Word with fresh eyes. Through that, I began to discover truths that set me free from burdens I had carried for years.

Tradition Can't Replace Revelation

It is essential that we read the Word of God for ourselves. I've encountered pastors who genuinely believe that laypeople can't understand the Bible without their interpretation—and that is simply not true. While God has indeed given us apostles, prophets, evangelists, pastors, and teachers to equip the saints for the work of ministry (Ephesians 4:11–12), that doesn't mean untitled believers are incapable of understanding Scripture on their own. Every born-again believer has Holy Spirit dwelling within. He doesn't just comfort us—He teaches us. Jesus called Him the Spirit of Truth, who leads us into all truth (John 16:13).

Jesus didn't rebuke the religious leaders of His day because they lacked Scripture knowledge. He rebuked them because their manmade traditions had replaced true obedience. They honored God with their lips, but their hearts were far from Him (Matthew 15:8–9). Unfortunately, the same thing is still happening in some churches today. Manmade traditions—like rigid dress codes, performance-based acceptance, hierarchical leadership that discourages questions, or equating emotional hype with spiritual depth—often take precedence over what matters to the heart of the Father.

I've learned that if I neglect studying the Bible for myself, I open the door to all kinds of things—legalism, cultural Christianity, and even spiritual manipulation. I could potentially start relying on what sounds good or feel familiar, instead of anchoring myself in what's true. When I chose to make Scripture a priority and invited Holy Spirit to illuminate it, everything shifted. I began to build my life on the unshakable foundation of Jesus Christ. I started to recognize the difference between truth and error, between grace and works, and between God's heart and human tradition. And as I did, I didn't just gain more knowledge—I began to grow in a real, thriving relationship with Him.

Learning to Listen

Listening to teaching can be a challenge sometimes, especially for someone like me who's used to doing a lot of talking! But, as I've learned to slow down and truly listen, I've noticed something. We all carry perspectives shaped by our experiences, and sometimes, those perspectives can influence how we interpret the Word and where we think others are spiritually.

The Bible is not a random collection of quotes or moral slogans. It's a living, God-breathed story filled with real people, real moments, and real lessons. It's meant to teach and transform us, not to be used as a grab bag of verses we apply rigidly to support personal opinions or expectations. And yet, it's easy—often unintentionally—reduced to that. Sometimes we take sincere insights and unintentionally turn them into standards for everyone else.

It's human nature to relate Scripture to our own journey and then assume it must apply the same way to others. But, while we can learn from all of God's Word, we must be careful not to project our personal convictions onto others, especially without knowing what's really going on in their hearts. Only God sees the full picture. What He's working out in one person's life may look very different in someone else's, even if the principle is the same.

For example, when Jesus told the rich young ruler to sell everything and follow Him (Luke 18:18–23), He wasn't giving a universal command for all believers to give up their possessions. He was addressing what was holding *that man* back in his heart. When we don't keep the Spirit and context in view, we risk misapplying Scripture or placing burdens where God never intended them.

This is why we need humility, discernment, and a deep reliance on the Holy Spirit—not just to know Scripture, but to understand the context and to apply it rightly. It's not about having all the answers. It's about walking in love, listening well, and trusting that God is at work in others, just as He is in us.

From Ritual to True Bible Study

Studying God's Word is not a daily ritual to check off a list—it's an invitation to grow in the grace and knowledge of our Lord and Savior Jesus Christ (2 Peter 3:18). The Word of God is valuable—more than gold, more than anything this world can offer. Church once taught me the importance of daily devotionals, and while that had its place, God began to teach me the value of *quality* time in His Word. It wasn't about opening my Bible at the same time every day—it was about consistently seeking Him and allowing Holy Spirit to make His Word come alive in my heart. When I gave the Word space to speak, it began to shape my thoughts, change my heart, and guide how I lived. It became more than a habit; it became life to me.

Reflection and Response

Ask yourself:
- Why do I read the Word—relationship or routine?
- Am I slowing down to truly hear God when I read?
- What verse recently spoke to me—and why?

A Prayer for Understanding God's Word

Father,

Thank You for giving me Your Word. I ask that You help me to understand it— not just with my mind, but with my heart. Teach me truth, Lord. Help me to read Your Word in the right context, led by Your Spirit. Strip away any traditional teachings or mindsets that keep me from receiving the truth You want me to know.

According to John 17:17, Sanctify me by Your Word, for Your Word is truth. Help me to see your word not as a rule book but as a living invitation to know You more deeply. Renew my mind through the truth of Your Word and transform my heart, so that my life brings honor to You in everything I do.

In Jesus' name, Amen.

Chapter 6: Holy Spirit: Our Teacher and Guide

When I rededicated my life to Christ, I heard about Holy Spirit—but I didn't really *know* Him. I knew He was a person, but I didn't know Him as a companion. I was taught, but I didn't understand. So, I lived most of my early walk with Father trying to do things in my own strength—reading the Bible without understanding, trying to change without power, and wondering why my relationship with Father felt distant.

It wasn't until I encountered Holy Spirit personally that I began to realize that He wasn't just *with* me—He was God's active presence *in* me. He wasn't just there to comfort me in hard times—He was there to lead me, teach me, and empower me every single day.

The Spirit Wasn't Optional—He Was Promised

"But the Advocate, the Holy Spirit, whom the Father will send in my name, will teach you all things and will remind you of everything I have said to you." — John 14:26 (NIV)

Jesus didn't leave His disciples with a book, a church building, or a set of religious rituals. He left them with Holy Spirit. The Spirit isn't an "extra" for elite born again believers. He is the source of life and power for all believers. Jesus said it was actually *better* for Him to leave so Holy Spirit could come (John 16:7). That means what the Spirit brings is not just helpful—He is essential.

The Spirit Brings Revelation of the Word

I read the Bible religiously yet still missed its power. But when Holy Spirit began to teach me, the Word became alive. Verses I've read many times suddenly spoke to my heart. I began to connect truth to my life in ways I never saw before. I began to see the error of my thinking not just from wrong teaching but my own misunderstanding.

"But when he, the Spirit of truth, comes, he will guide you into all the truth." — John 16:13 (NIV)

Holy Spirit is not just your emotional helper—He is your truth guide. He illuminates Scripture. He exposes lies. He confirms Father's voice. Without Him, it's easy to fall into dead tradition or self-interpretation.

The Spirit Empowers Transformation

"You, however, are not in the realm of the flesh but are in the realm of the Spirit, if indeed the Spirit of Father lives in you." — Romans 8:9 (NIV)

We were never meant to live the life of a believer in Christ in our own strength. That's why so many believers are exhausted trying to overcome sin, change habits, and walk in holiness without the power of the Spirit. This was definitely me. Thank God for teaching me to trust His Spirit in me to help me to grow in areas that I had struggled in for so long. The more I trusted God's Spirit in me, the more freedom I begin to experience from sin, manmade rules, religious ritual, and church traditions.

Holy Spirit empowers us to overcome sin (Romans 8:13), bear spiritual fruit (Galatians 5:22–23), walk in truth and be led, not driven by flesh (Romans 8:14). He doesn't just call us to transformation—He enables it. He lets us know when we need to make a course correction.

Some people interpret John 16:8 to mean that the Holy Spirit convicts believers of sin. But when we look at the verse in context, and in its original language, a different picture emerges. The verse reads:

"When He [the Holy Spirit] comes, He will convict *the world* of sin, and of righteousness, and of judgment" (John 16:8, NIV, italics added). The Greek word translated "convict" is *elegchō,* which means to expose, bring to light, or prove wrong—specifically to confront someone with the truth (Strong's Concordance, G1651). In this passage, Jesus is speaking about the Spirit's role in the lives of unbelievers, not believers. Verse 9 clarifies the focus: *the sin being exposed is their unbelief in Him* (John 16:9, NIV). So, John 16:8 is about the Holy Spirit awakening the world to their need for Jesus—not about correcting Christians.

Most churches don't use the word "convict" to imply condemnation or guilt; they typically mean the Holy Spirit shows us when we're wrong so we can grow. But by applying the definition from John 16:8 to believers, the Church often unintentionally misuses the verse. For those in Christ, Scripture is clear: "There is now no condemnation for those who are in Christ Jesus" (Romans 8:1, NIV). The Holy Spirit doesn't "convict" believers in the sense of exposing sin to prove them wrong or shame them. Instead, He gently teaches, corrects, leads, and reminds us of who we are in Christ (see John 14:26; Romans 8:14; Hebrews 12:6–11, NIV). He disciplines us as a loving Father—not a courtroom judge. True spiritual correction is about restoration, not guilt. So, while the Holy Spirit absolutely guides believers away from sin, we honor Scripture best by using accurate language: the Spirit corrects, guides, and leads us into truth—not convicts in the way John 16:8 describes.

Recognizing the Spirit's Leading

Being led by the Spirit doesn't always feel "super spiritual" to me. Sometimes, it's just a quiet nudge in my heart. Other times, it's a moment when something in Scripture suddenly makes sense in a way it didn't before. And then there are those times when I feel a gentle uneasiness about a decision or relationship—it's not loud, but I know it's the Holy Spirit trying to get my attention. He never condemns me or shames me. That's not how He works. Instead, He lovingly shows me the places in my life that aren't in line with God's truth—not to make me feel guilty, but to help me walk in the freedom I've already been given. He reminds me of who I am in Christ, and when I'm not living like it, He brings it to light in the most tender, honest way. That's how He deals with me. I can't speak for others.

I've found that the more time I spend in God's presence and in His Word, the more clearly I recognize the Spirit's voice. He teaches me, corrects me, and helps me grow—but never through fear or pressure ... always through truth and grace. He never accuses me. He simply invites me to walk in the light, to walk in truth, and to remember who I am. And I'm learning to trust that He will always lead me toward freedom, humility, and holiness—never away from it.

Don't Outsource the Holy Spirit

I didn't always realize it, but for a long time, I was relying more on my pastor or a favorite speaker than I was on the Holy Spirit. Their messages encouraged me and helped me grow, but I started to see that I was looking to them for answers I should have been seeking from God Himself. I am grateful that Father met me where I was but didn't leave me there in that state of dependency on man.

The truth is, no matter how gifted, anointed, or wise a leader may be, they were never meant to replace the role of the Holy Spirit in my life. He's been given to each of us personally—not just to pastors or spiritual leaders, but to every believer. He desires to speak, guide, and lead me just as clearly as He does anyone else.

Pastors and teachers are a vital part of the Body of Christ. We need their wisdom, covering, and spiritual maturity. But when we neglect our personal walk with God—when we don't study, pray, or seek Him for ourselves—we unintentionally put an unfair burden on our leaders. We expect them to hear from God *for* us, carry our spiritual growth, and have all the answers. And when things don't go the way we hoped, we often turn around and blame the very people who were simply doing what God called them to do. That kind of pressure can deeply wound pastors who are sincerely trying to shepherd God's people with integrity. It's not their job to carry what we're responsible for cultivating.

While God absolutely speaks through His appointed leaders, He also speaks directly to us. I had to learn to slow down, listen, and trust that He would lead me—not apart from my leaders, but alongside the guidance they give. The same Spirit who empowers our pastors is the One who lives in us—and He is faithful to lead each of us every step of the way.

"But you have received the Holy Spirit, and he lives within you, so you don't need anyone to teach you what is true. For the Spirit teaches you everything you need to know…" — 1 John 2:27 (NLT)

This Scripture doesn't mean we reject teachers—it means we don't become dependent on man at the expense of listening to God. While 1 John 2:27 emphasizes that believers have Holy Spirit and therefore do not need anyone to teach them, this does not negate the role of spiritual leaders in the Church. In context, John is warning against false teachers and affirming that Holy Spirit enables believers to discern truth and remain rooted in Christ. However, Ephesians 4:11–12 reveals that Christ Himself gave apostles, prophets, evangelists, pastors, and teachers to the Church—not as spiritual gatekeepers, but as servants who equip the saints for ministry and help build up the Body of Christ. These leaders are not meant to replace the Spirit's guidance, but to complement it. While Holy Spirit often teaches us through God's Word, He also teaches us through others, giving them wisdom and sharing some of their experiences to deepen our understanding. God never intended for us to grow in isolation; rather,

He designed us to thrive in community, where the Spirit works both within us and among us.

Reflection and Response

Ask yourself:

- Have I been trying to live the Christian life without the Holy Spirit?
- Do I invite Him to lead me consistently—or only when I'm in trouble?
- Am I willing to slow down, listen, and follow—even when it's uncomfortable?
- Have I put my trust more in man than Holy Spirit?

A Prayer to Be Led by the Holy Spirit

Father,

Thank You for giving me Your Holy Spirit to live within me. I ask that You help me learn to be led by Him in all things. Teach me to recognize Your voice and become familiar with the gentle leading of Your Spirit. Help me to humble myself and fully acknowledge my need for Your presence and guidance in my life.

Even though I have Your Spirit to guide me, help me to not ignore those whom You speak through to reach me. At the same time, help me to not hold the voices of others higher than the voice of Your Spirit.

Grow in me the fruit of the Spirit—love, joy, peace, patience, kindness, goodness, faithfulness, gentleness, and self-control. Let Your Spirit transform me from the inside out, shaping my heart, renewing my mind, and aligning my life with Your will.

In Jesus' name, Amen.

Chapter 7: The Unfolding of Purpose

When Purpose Felt Distant

With all I was doing in church, I still felt inadequate. I watched others speak with confidence about their purpose and calling, while I struggled in silence. Everyone around me seemed to have clarity—like they had received a personal invitation from Heaven to step into their destiny. Me? I had no clue.

From a young believer, it had been ingrained in me that I needed to seek God for my calling. I heard that if I didn't know what I was called to do, I'd waste my time on earth. I thought I might die with my gifts still inside me, unused and unfulfilled. I cried out to God, desperately longing for an answer. The silence felt deafening. No matter how deeply I prayed, I heard nothing about a calling. That silence became a weight I carried for years—until one unexpected day, Father spoke.

The Whisper That Changed Everything

I heard it in my spirit—quiet, yet powerful: "If you would simply walk with Me day by day, you will naturally walk into your calling." Those words unlocked something deep within me. They peeled back a layer of fear and striving that had wrapped itself around my identity. I didn't need to chase a calling anymore. I simply needed to walk with my Father. That revelation brought freedom. As I walked with Him in everyday life, He began to reveal things to me—naturally and without force. I would step into assignments He placed before me without the endless searching or stress. I was able to accomplish those assignments successfully because He was with me, and it seems I have always had the right people in my life, as if Heaven had orchestrated their presence in advance.

The Father Who Chose Me – The Best Mom

I think of my dad, Eugene Johnson Sr. He met my mother while she was pregnant with me and chose to love me as his own. I never once doubted that he was my father. Even when he eventually told me he wasn't my biological dad, it hardly mattered—because love already embraced me. He was my daddy. In a world where families are often divided, I was blessed with wonderful parents and siblings. My mother is such a wonderful friend to me. I can talk to her about anything. I almost embarrass her at times with my transparency. How many daughters can truly say that? That wasn't always the case until God healed my heart. She encourages me in my marriage, in my role as a mother, and in my walk with God. My family is one of my greatest treasures.

Divine Connections

I think of my dear sister Lisa Evans, who stuck by me in the ministry and stood beside me as my maid of honor. Her life taught me one simple but powerful lesson: *"Press on."* Those two words became a lifeline. They reminded me that challenges weren't stop signs, just opportunities to lean on God and keep moving forward.

I think of Mom and Dad Dotson, mentors who loved me for me. I practically lived in their home on Sundays. They showed me what godly mentorship, friendship, parenting, integrity, and leadership looked like in action. When they moved to Texas, I thought I would be lost. But, through them, I learned to let Christ be my anchor.

There is Mom Qualls, who entered my life through the tutoring center where I enrolled my goddaughter. Working for her is where I cut my teeth in youth development and began to understand the power of education. That season shaped the kind of mother I would become. To this day, she is one of my greatest cheerleaders.

The Marriage That Endured

Before and during my marriage, God placed people in our lives who poured into us at just the right moments. The marriage ministry at Calvary Revival Church was a lifeline. Bishop Courtney McBath taught us the spiritual foundation of covenant. Pastor David Martin and Pastors Mark and Dawn Lawrence were instrumental in helping my husband and me navigate critical moments in our marriage. God used these great pastors to sustain something He had joined together.

Kingdom Family and the Power of Community

God has surrounded me with a Kingdom family—people from my place of fellowship and others who've impacted me deeply. I think of my many faithful sisters who have walked alongside me. I think of the friend who God used to teach me the beauty and balance of enduring in a genuine friendship despite the ups and downs. Everyone needs Godly friends. I think about Aunt Tonya Everett. When I first got married, I instantly became a mom because my husband was a single father with girls. Then the baby boys came along. Aunt Tonya was truly a godsend. She was always there when I needed her, becoming one of my greatest support systems along with Uncle Marty.

I also think about my ex-boss, Victor Pickett. He understood my devotion to my family. Despite all that he needed from me in corporate America, he never stood in the way of me putting my family first. He may not realize how much that meant to me, but it was invaluable, especially in a world today where most employers could care less about your family and only focus on the bottom line. But Victor was different. He was a man devoted to his own family as well, and I thank God for him.

I think of my Word and Worship Center family. Through this Kingdom Community, I've discovered many of my faults and many of my gifts. I've established healthy and Godly relationships, and I've

45

grown in leadership, love, service, and truth. I know beyond a shadow of a doubt that my pastors James and Denise Wheeler love me. God used my Kingdom family to help me break through walls I didn't even know existed. Every relationship was necessary for me to become who I am to walk in my purpose and my calling.

The Difference Between Purpose and Calling

One of the most life-changing revelations God gave me was understanding the difference between purpose and calling. In church, these words are often used interchangeably, but they aren't the same. Our purpose is universal—it's to know God, love Him, and glorify Him with our lives. Revelation 4:11 reminds us that we were created by His will, for His pleasure. That means our very existence brings joy to God. Before we ever do anything for Him, He finds delight in who we are to Him.

Our calling, then, is the specific role, assignment, or area of influence God gives us to walk out that purpose in a unique way. Some people do receive very specific callings—like being a pastor, teacher, or missionary. But for many, the focus isn't about discovering a title; it's about living in a way that pleases God wherever He's places us. If we can't please Him in it, we shouldn't be doing it. Whether you're leading a ministry or raising a family, writing a book or working a 9–5 job, the question isn't always *what* you're doing, but *why*—and *who* you're doing it for. Purpose gives meaning to calling, and calling becomes an expression of purpose. Once I understood that, I no longer felt trapped in titles or tasks. My calling became less about "what" and more about whom I was doing it for. This freed me to say yes to God fully—and to walk boldly into spaces I once avoided. It was not always comfortable stepping out into certain areas of ministry, but I trusted Him to lead me by His Spirit, I could do it. However, stepping into some spaces was extra challenging.

Learning to Lead in Freedom

Even when I sensed my calling, I avoided it—because that calling meant leadership, and I dreaded it. My past experiences with church leadership had left a bitter taste. It felt like there were so many unnecessary requirements. Church often created so many ministries, and leading those ministries came with obligations I didn't always believe in. I was expected to attend functions that I didn't want to be bothered with. I believe in serving God wholeheartedly, but I don't believe that people should be required to attend every function someone else deems necessary. One of the hardest things for me to navigate was the line between what God was asking of me and what church leaders were asking. Sometimes leaders would say, "God told me to fast," and suddenly, the entire team was expected to join in. Fasting is good—sometimes necessary—but I need to know why I'm fasting, not just follow along blindly.

I'm so grateful for Mom Dotson, who taught me never to let anyone in ministry put more on my plate than what God has given me to carry—not even the pastor. Her words continue to guide me even now in ministry. It's only by the grace of God that I've learned to balance honoring my leaders while also having the confidence to graciously decline tasks that God hasn't assigned to me. There was a time when, deep down, I worried about what others, especially leaders, would think of me if I didn't comply. But now, I've come to understand that what matters most is what God says. His approval is my peace.

Leadership is not about fulfilling a list of tasks that someone else assigns in the name of God. True godly leadership is about representing Him in such a way that others are drawn closer to Him through your example. As the Word says, "Whatever you do, do it heartily, as to the Lord and not to men" (Colossians 3:23). If I'm entrusted to lead, I will give my best to honor God and serve His people. But I don't want to be bound to traditions and obligations that have nothing to do what Father has called me to.

Training is necessary. I understand that. But I learned that leadership should never become a burden that pulls me away from the freedom God is teaching me to walk in. "It is for freedom that Christ has set us free. Stand firm, then, and do not let yourselves be burdened again by a yoke of slavery" (Galatians 5:1). I'm grateful that I was able to sit down with my current pastors and have an honest, heartfelt conversation about my concerns. I want to follow God fully—not be trapped by man's expectations. Thankfully, having loving leaders with servant's hearts encouraged me to step in more than I normally would. So, with a renewed heart, I was ready to move forward.

Ordained for Access

On September 1, 2024, I was ordained—not as a pastor, because I know that is not my calling—but as a minister. I don't place much weight on the title itself. The word "minister" means servant, and that's a role all believers should walk in. But, God showed me something bigger: The title wasn't for my benefit—it was for access.

In this world, even in church, people get bound by titles. Sometimes, without a title, you're not even allowed through the door. So, God branded me with a title, not for status, but for Him. He has put me in the position to have access to places I otherwise wouldn't be allowed into—so that I can go in, speak His truth, and walk back out.

My calling is to be an instrument in His hands to help others walk in freedom from traditions and manmade rules that have made His Word ineffective in their lives and ministries.

The Joy of Pleasing the Father

There is no greater joy or privilege than pleasing the Father, serving Him, and serving others for Him. Every time I've obeyed Him,

He has made my efforts successful. Not because of my strength, but because I stayed focused on my purpose—to bring Him pleasure.

My beginning wasn't a lightning strike or a voice from a burning bush. It was a quiet, steady walk—one foot in front of the other, hand in hand with my Father. And in that walk, I found freedom. I found clarity. I found the beginning to truly live.

Reflection and Response

Ask yourself:
- When has purpose felt distant in my life, and how did God meet me there?
- How has understanding the difference between purpose and calling changed the way I live or lead?
- What does it look like for me to please the Father with joy rather than pressure?

Prayer of Thankfulness for Clarity, Growth, and Godly Leadership

Father,

Thank You for calling me, for choosing me, and for being patient with me when I resisted what You had placed inside of me. I am so grateful that You didn't give up on me, even when I tried to run from the very thing You created me to do. Thank You for helping me understand that my purpose and my calling are not burdens, but gifts—assignments designed by Your hand for Your glory and my growth.

Thank You for the people You have placed along my journey—those who poured into me, encouraged me, challenged me, and even those who made me uncomfortable—because all of them have helped shape who I am today. I see now that nothing was wasted. You used every voice, every situation, and every lesson to bring clarity to my purpose and maturity to my spirit.

Lord, I thank You for giving me a heart that desires to please You above all else. Thank You for removing the fear of man and breaking the chains of religious pressure. I'm grateful for a right heart attitude to lead—not to control or impress, but to serve, represent You well, and point others back to You.

Help me to keep walking in the freedom You've given me. Help me to be a leader who is led by Your Spirit and not by tradition. Help me make decisions that flow from intimacy with You, not obligation to man. May my life—and my service— always reflect Your grace, Your truth, and Your love.

In Jesus' name, Amen.

Chapter 8: The Trap of Tradition

It's possible to be in church every Sunday, serve faithfully, and still feel far from Father. That was my story for years. I equated religious activity with spiritual depth, thinking that doing more meant I was growing. But over time, I realized I was more connected to a system than to the Savior. Don't confuse what I'm saying. I was still saved ... just a spiritual work-a-holic. I wasn't alone. Many sincere believers live bound by rules, routines, and rituals passed down by tradition—but never question if those things are drawing them closer to Father or just keeping them busy. Somewhere along the way, manmade rules became a substitute for relationship.

There are many things we do in church that feel normal to us— patterns we follow because they've been passed down over time. Some traditions aren't necessarily wrong or harmful; in fact, many of them help create order, consistency, and unity during our gatherings. But it's important to recognize that some of what we've come to view as "the way church is done" is rooted more in tradition than in direct biblical instruction.

The typical Sunday structure—praise and worship, announcements, offering, and then the sermon—can be a beautiful and effective way to gather. It brings flow and rhythm, and order matters. Without it, a service can easily become chaotic or distracting. But we also must be careful not to equate the structure itself with spiritual power. I've visited ministries that didn't follow the traditional format—and I was deeply impacted by the word. Some didn't have a formal praise and worship segment. Some didn't take up a public offering. And yet, the Word of God was taught with clarity, power, and authority. The Spirit of God moved freely, and the people were fully engaged—not because of routine, but because their hearts were open and hungry.

Those experiences reminded me that while structure can be helpful, God is not confined by it. What truly matters is His presence, the truth of His Word, and hearts ready to receive. Whether a service follows a familiar format or not, the goal should always be the same: to glorify God, to build up His people, and to make room for Him to move as He wills. For example, many believe that singing songs of praise and worship is "required" to prepare our hearts or to create an atmosphere for God to move. While Psalm 100:4 encourages us to "enter His gates with thanksgiving and His courts with praise," this verse reflects a beautiful spiritual principle—approaching God with reverence and gratitude—not a rigid formula for how every service must begin.

Singing unto the Lord is both biblical and beautiful. It's a heartfelt expression of love, adoration, and honor toward God, and it can be a powerful way to engage with His presence. But problems arise when even something as good as praise and worship becomes a tool for pressure or judgment. Sadly, when people don't respond with loud singing, clapping, or outward expressions of praise, they're sometimes scolded from the pulpit or made to feel spiritually disconnected. But what about the quiet worshipper—the one who simply lifts their hands, closes their eyes, or stands in silent reverence with their heart fully focused on God? True worship is not about performance or emotional display; it's about the posture of the heart—and that's something only God can see. Praise and worship should be an invitation, not a demand—a sacred space where each person is free to honor God sincerely, in the way they are led, as long as they are not disruptive. Everyone connects with God differently, and I try not to measure others by my own expressions.

What is Worship

In the body of Christ, there are many interpretations of what worship truly is. Biblically speaking, worship is far more than music, posture, or emotion. It is a lifestyle of reverence and surrender to God. The word most commonly translated as "worship" in the New Testament is the Greek word proskuneō, which means to bow down, to kneel, or to show reverence and adoration. In Romans 12:1, Paul gives us a fuller picture of biblical worship. "Therefore, I urge you, brothers and sisters, in view of God's mercy, to offer your bodies as a living sacrifice, holy and pleasing to God—this is your true and proper worship." This verse makes it clear—worship is how we live, not just what we do during a service.

Some people have been in church so long that they've become conditioned to lift their hands or sing at the "right" moments, but that doesn't necessarily mean they're connecting with God. And on the flip side, some people may appear distant or disengaged during worship time, but they live in deep communion with God daily. Worship flows out of intimacy with God, not performance or routine. Worship is not measured by volume or movement, but by the sincerity of the heart.

For those who connect deeply through music—who lift their hands, close their eyes, and reflect on God's goodness during worship—it can feel strange or even disappointing to see others standing still or seemingly unresponsive. Honestly, I've had moments where I couldn't understand why anyone wouldn't worship God, especially when He has been so good to us. Even if He did nothing more than send His Son to save us, that alone is reason enough to give Him glory without holding back. But I've learned to be careful—not to judge or assume. It's not my place to draw conclusions about someone's relationship with God based on a few minutes of observation. I don't know what's going on in their heart or what they may be wrestling with at that moment. Maybe they're distracted, struggling, or simply connecting with God in a quieter way. My focus

53

should remain on honoring God myself—and trusting that He sees and knows every heart better than I ever could.

Sometimes the music itself can be a distraction. Over the years there have been times when the music in church didn't resonate with me. Some songs felt too self-centered or emotionally driven. But my wise mentor taught me that even if I don't connect with a particular song, I can still worship because God is still worthy. Music isn't the core of worship. It's just a tool. I can tune out the song and tune in to my Father in Heaven. That wasn't easy at first—especially when I found the lyrics distracting—but over time, I've learned to focus my heart regardless of the music. Some songs draw me in instantly—especially the ones that speak directly about who God is. Those are the songs that stir my spirit. I'm less drawn to songs that dwell on personal testimonies or struggles because not everyone shares the same experience. I'd rather focus on the greatness of God, His faithfulness, and His goodness. I know I've been delivered, so there's no need for me to rehearse the brokenness. I want to sing about the One who *saved a wretch like me.* No matter the song, I will bless the Lord.

At its core, worship is not about us. It's about God. It's about ascribing worth to Him simply for who He is. In that process, there is such *beauty* and *value*—because worship opens a sacred space where we commune with God. For those who seem disengaged during worship, they may be missing a beautiful opportunity in that moment to connect with the heart of the Father—not because they don't love Him, but because something may be keeping them from entering in fully during that time. That doesn't mean they aren't walking with God in their daily lives, but it may mean that they're bypassing a moment of closeness God is inviting them into right then and there.

Someone dear to me said it's encouraging to the pastors when they see the congregation engaged in worship. I believe it blesses their hearts to see people engaged in honoring God. Still, as much as we rejoice in corporate worship, we must remember that even in a room full of people, worship is ultimately personal. It is between the individual and God. And while it's powerful to worship together as the body of Christ, each person still must choose to lift their own heart to the One who is worthy. That's between them and Father.

Jesus kept it simple. He didn't need a praise team to set the atmosphere. He didn't wait for the right song or the perfect lighting. He simply showed up—and people followed. They sat wherever they were, ready to listen. No opening act. No emotional buildup. Just hungry hearts and open ears.

Can you imagine walking into a morning or evening service where people are already leaning in, eager to hear the Word—without needing a production to stir them or music to prepare them? Now, don't get me wrong. I'm not knocking the praise and worship portion of a service. Worship through music is powerful, and some ministries don't include it out of routine or obligation. They simply enjoy the opportunity to come together as a Kingdom Family to lift up our God. There is beauty in singing together as the Body of Christ. But, we must be careful not to become so programmed that we rely on the routine of Sunday morning just to feel close to God.

It is important that we live with an internal longing for God— a hunger that doesn't depend on external prompts. We shouldn't need the right song or the right atmosphere to worship. Believers should be moved by the mere thought of His presence, stirred by the truth of His Word. He shows up when we show up because He lives in us.

I pray this for all believers—that we would crave His presence, not the performance; that we would hunger for His Word, whether there's a choir or complete quiet. May our worship be sincere, our ears attentive, and our hearts ready—simply because we love Him.

Loose Lips Can Create Human Rules

"These people honor me with their lips, but their hearts are far from me. They worship me in vain; their teachings are merely human rules." — *Matthew 15:8– 9 (NIV)*

Jesus wasn't impressed by outward devotion that lacked inward connection. The Pharisees had perfected the appearance of righteousness but missed the heart of Father. They built fences of oral laws around Father's commands to avoid breaking them, but in doing so, they elevated man's voice above Father's. Tradition in itself isn't wrong—but when it becomes a replacement for relationship, or when it contradicts Scripture, it becomes dangerous.

Over time, some churches have created rules that, while well-intentioned, have ended up replacing the truth of God's Word. These manmade standards can become a burden and create an atmosphere of legalism rather than freedom. Some churches teach that women must not wear pants, makeup, or jewelry—as if holiness can be measured by appearance. Others forbid going to the movies, listening to certain types of music, or even celebrating holidays. In some cases, people are judged for having tattoos, piercings, or certain hairstyles. Even traditions like requiring a specific style of worship, insisting on long altar calls, or expecting people to dress in formal attire for service can subtly teach that outward conformity equals spiritual maturity. But Jesus never taught these things. In fact, He often rebuked the religious leaders for placing heavy burdens on people—rules that God never required (Matthew 23:4).

Now, to be clear, there is such a thing as appropriateness when it comes to dress, whether it is on your job, in public, or gathering with others to worship. Modesty, respect, and thoughtfulness matter. But at the same time, we must remember that when people first come to Christ, they often come wearing whatever they have. And that's okay. While the phrase "come as you are" doesn't appear word-for-word in Scripture, the heart of the gospel invites all to come—to bring their brokenness, their struggles, and yes, even their imperfect presentation. The change happens after the encounter—not before. And even then, many changes happen gradually, not overnight.

True holiness begins in the heart, and real transformation flows from the inside out by the work of the Holy Spirit—not through external rules or pressure. When I rededicated my life to the Lord, I immediately sensed a shift in what I desired to watch or listen to and made changes in my entertainment choices. But when it came to how I dressed, that didn't change right away. God was working with me patiently, addressing deeper things first. He didn't force change from the outside in—He gently led me into truth over time. In the same way, when someone is new to the faith and hasn't yet grown in intimacy with God, we may feel a desire to guide them. But we must be careful not to impose rules or expectations that God Himself hasn't yet revealed to their hearts. Correction, when needed, should come from a place of love, not control—always pointing them back to relationship with Father, not religious performance. That's why I've come to understand that when tradition takes the place of truth, we risk reducing church to performance instead of relationship. Real growth happens through intimacy with God, not by conforming to outward expectations.

"So then, just as you received Christ Jesus as Lord, continue to live your lives in him, rooted and built up in him, strengthened in the faith… and not according to human tradition." — Colossians 2:6–8 (paraphrased)

Paul warned the early church not to let hollow traditions pull them away from the simplicity and purity of devotion to Christ. Today, we need that same warning. Father is not interested in how perfectly we perform our traditions—He desires hearts that are rooted in truth. And we cannot thrive in a relationship where control, fear, or human agendas dominate.

How Believers Fall into the Trap

The trap is often subtle. Some believers begin to follow church culture instead of kingdom truth, quoting phrases that sound spiritual but aren't scriptural. Sometimes, we adopt patterns simply because "that's how it's always been done," without pausing to ask if it's truly Spirit-led. Over time, we can become more hesitant to step away from tradition than we are to pursue fresh direction from God. And without realizing it, we may pass those same patterns on to others—not out of malice, but because it's all we've known. In some cases, long-standing traditions—though originally rooted in good intentions—can become wrapped in guilt or fear, such as "Don't question leadership," "Don't miss church or you'll fall away," or "Tithe or you'll be cursed." While these statements may sound righteous, if they're not clearly supported by Scripture and led by the Spirit, they can unintentionally produce pressure, performance, and spiritual exhaustion rather than deeper intimacy with God.

A practical example of this is when church involvement begins to feel like a checklist. A person might attend faithfully, serve, tithe, and participate in every activity—yet still feel spiritually dry or distant. That's not necessarily the fault of the church or leadership. In many cases, pastors sincerely do their best to lead with love and truth. But if we as individuals begin to "do church" instead of genuinely seeking to know the Father, our actions can become obligations instead of expressions of relationship. Instead of asking, "Father, what are You leading me to do?", we often default to, "What am I supposed to do to be a good Christian?" That's the quiet trap—replacing Spirit-led obedience with routine. Real transformation always starts with relationship, not religious repetition.

Manmade Rules Builds Walls. Jesus Breaks Chains.

Religious systems often pile on rules that Jesus never gave. Some teachings may sound spiritual, but if they're used to control, manipulate, or condemn, they're just man-made chains. They are not rooted in the full counsel of Scripture.

To be fair, many pastors don't teach these things with harmful intent. In many cases, they're simply passing on what was taught to them—ideas that have become deeply woven into their understanding of faith. It's not that they don't know the Word; it's that long-standing tradition can sometimes influence how the Word is interpreted. Instead of filtering what they were taught through Scripture, they may unintentionally filter Scripture through what they were taught.

This isn't always about trying to control people. Often, it's about what they sincerely believe to be right—what they feel strongly convicted about. In this context, *conviction* doesn't mean guilt or shame. It means a deeply held belief that something is true or necessary. But when those beliefs are based more on tradition than on the full truth of God's Word, it can lead to teachings that sound spiritual yet keep people bound rather than free.

One common example of this is the belief that missing church—especially on a Sunday or during midweek Bible study—means God is no longer important to you. There's a wall of teaching around this, where commitment to a building is often equated with commitment to God. But the truth is, God doesn't measure our devotion by a calendar. Even if someone invites me to do something fun on a Sunday morning or Bible study night, saying yes wouldn't upset God. God isn't mad if you have to work on Sunday. Our Father is not threatened by rest, relationships, jobs or recreation. In fact, sometimes He uses those very moments to open doors for ministry. Just don't neglect what is important to Him.

This is true not just for congregants but for pastors too. It's unrealistic—and unfair—to expect our leaders to be present every Sunday, every Bible study, and at every event without pause. Pastors are human, and they also need rest, refreshment, and time with their own families. Yet some people pull on them selfishly, expecting them to always be "on" or available. That pressure isn't just exhausting—it's unhealthy. If we truly love our leaders, we'll honor their humanity, respect their rhythms, and trust that God can speak and move even when they take time to rest.

I have missed Bible study a few times. One particular evening, I was on my way to Bible study when I suddenly began to feel sick. I turned the car around and went home. As I pulled into the driveway, I saw my sons playing basketball with the neighbor's son. Just as I got out of the car, the neighbor's son jumped too high to make a shot and hit his head on the rim. He came down bleeding. I immediately called 911 and stepped into action. Here's the thing—*the moment I ran to help, the sickness I had felt was gone*, and it didn't come back.

What would have happened had I not been there? What if I had ignored what I felt because I believed that being at Bible study was the only way to please God? That night reminded me: ministry doesn't just happen in the building. Sometimes the most powerful ministry happens when we're willing to follow God *outside* the expected places. You never know when a moment of presence becomes a moment of purpose.

Now, this doesn't mean that gathering with other believers isn't important—it is. Fellowship is a vital part of spiritual growth, accountability, and encouragement. But I'll go more into that in Chapter 12. The key point here is that attending church doesn't define your closeness with God, and missing a scheduled service doesn't mean you're falling away. God's presence isn't confined to pews and pulpits.

Jesus came to break every system that keeps people from the Father. He tore the veil. He fulfilled the law—perfectly satisfying every requirement—so we could live free from the weight of guilt and fear. He invites us to walk in the freedom of grace and truth, not religious performance. His Spirit is not confined to Sundays or sanctuaries. He moves through everyday obedience, spontaneous interruptions, and our willingness to say yes to His prompting—whether we're in church, at work, or at play.

God is far more interested in intimacy than performance. And when we walk in that freedom, we stop trying to prove our devotion through rigid routines and start living it through love, availability, and trust. Ministry happens in church pews, yes—but it also happens in driveways, on sidewalks, on vacation, and in moments we didn't plan. When we follow the Spirit, *every moment* becomes holy ground.

Reflection and Response

Ask yourself:
- Where do I feel trapped by tradition?
- What religious expectations am I ready to release?
- How can I embrace freedom beyond routine?

Prayer to Be Free from Traditions

Father,

Open my eyes to any area where I've replaced Your voice with tradition. Help me to recognize and release every religious expectation that isn't from You. I don't want to go through the motions—I want a real, living relationship with You. Teach me by Your Word and lead me by Your Spirit.

As You show me truth, help me to grow in grace, not arrogance. Remind me that revelation from You does not make me spiritually superior. Keep my heart humble and tender toward others who may still be walking in traditions You've called me to release. Help me walk in freedom without becoming prideful or critical.

Teach me how to step away from man-made customs with confidence and peace, while still showing love and respect to those who continue in them. Instead of judging, help me to pray—fervently and sincerely—for Your people to experience the same freedom that You've given me. Freedom that draws us closer to Your heart, not just further from routines.

I surrender every false thing and every place where I've allowed tradition to take the place of truth. I return to You fully, hungry to be led by Your Spirit and rooted in Your grace.

In Jesus' name, Amen.

Chapter 9: Freedom in Christ
Breaking Religious Chains

I used to think freedom in Christ meant trying harder not to sin. I thought if I could follow all the rules, avoid every mistake, and meet everyone's expectations, then I'd finally feel free and accepted by Father. But no matter how hard I tried, I still felt bound—by guilt, by fear, by man's approval. My life was full of church activities but empty of real peace. I didn't realize I was still wearing chains, only now they were dressed in religious language. Then I read these words:

"It is for freedom that Christ has set us free. Stand firm, then, and do not let yourselves be burdened again by a yoke of slavery." (Galatians 5:1 NIV)

That verse shattered something in me. Christ didn't set me free so I could become a better performer. He set me free so I could live as His child, not a slave to unrighteousness. He doesn't want me bound by religious rituals, but in a healthy thriving relationship with Him.

True Freedom Through Christ

In the Biblical context, freedom means unbound to sin, legalism, or religious performance. Real freedom doesn't come through religious effort or self-help strategies—it comes through Jesus alone. The moment we are born again, He breaks the power of sin, shame, and spiritual death over us. Walking in that freedom begins with knowing the truth and then learning to live like people who are truly free. Some of us have been spiritually unlocked, yet we continue to live in the prison cell of old thinking. Sadly, much of this mindset isn't just from our life before Christ—it sometimes stems from what we were taught in church. In some cases, teaching jumps straight from salvation to "stop sinning," without ever laying the foundation of what it means to have a thriving relationship with the Father. Some people are given a list of dos and don'ts before they are even taught how to walk with God or what became available to them the moment they became His children. Freedom in Christ is not just about behavior changes—it's about identity, intimacy, and walking in the power and grace He has already given us.

In Romans 6, Paul addresses a critical misunderstanding that could arise from his teaching on grace. In the previous chapter, he declared that where sin increased, grace increased all the more. This powerful truth, however, could be misinterpreted to mean that continuing in sin somehow magnifies grace. Anticipating this distortion, Paul opens Romans 6 with a pointed question: "What shall we say then? Are we to continue in sin that grace may abound?" His response is swift and emphatic: "By no means!" Paul explains that those who are in Christ have died to sin and can no longer live under its dominion. Through baptism, believers are symbolically united with Christ in both His death and resurrection. Our old selves—once bound by the power of sin—have been crucified with Him. As a result, we are no longer slaves to sin, but alive to God. Paul uses the metaphor of slavery to highlight this transformation: before Christ, we lived under the rule of sin; now, we are empowered to live under grace, producing fruit that leads to life. Yet many believers still live as if they are bound. Moreover, they've been taught that because they struggle with sin, they must still be slaves to it. But slavery implies powerlessness—and that is no longer true for those who are in Christ. We aren't powerless. We just don't always walk in the power that has already been given to us. The reasons may vary.

We're not striving for freedom; we've been given freedom. The real challenge is learning to believe what's already true. If you think you're still a slave, you'll live like one—even when you've been set free. And when your mind is still aligned with bondage, your behavior will follow. That's often when many fall into religious striving, working to achieve what has already been provided through Christ.

I remember someone coming to the altar one day, asking me to pray and "ask God" for something on their behalf. In that moment, the Holy Spirit gently showed me that they weren't lacking the thing they were asking for—they just didn't know it had already been given to them. What they needed was confidence to receive what was already theirs in Christ, and trust that God would help them walk in it. That moment reminded me how easy it is to live as if we're still waiting on God, when in truth, He's already made provision—we just need eyes to see it and faith to receive it. I'm not talking about blab it and grab it. I'm talking about being loved and being made righteous through Christ without having to work or beg for it.

Struggling with sin isn't proof of defeat—it's evidence of new life. Before Christ, there was no struggle—just sin. Now, the Holy Spirit lives within us and won't allow us to be comfortable in what no longer fits our identity. The tension we feel is a sign of transformation, not condemnation. It's not about losing salvation, but about learning to walk in freedom from a sinful lifestyle. This is also where the chains of religion begin to break—not through fear or performance, but through *trust*. God doesn't call us forward through shame or guilt. He doesn't manipulate us with reminders of how bad we were to push us into service. Unfortunately, from some pulpits, we still hear these echoes—constant references to who we "used to be," as though guilt or comparison can motivate spiritual growth. But God doesn't operate that way. In Christ, we are free. We don't need to be defined by our past because that person no longer exists. As Romans 6:6–7 declares, "Our old self was crucified with Him… so that we would no longer be enslaved to sin, for the one who has died has been set free from sin." Because of this new identity—this relationship in which we are children of a great and loving God—freedom in Christ means we are no longer bound by the law to achieve righteousness, nor enslaved to sin. That truth doesn't make me want to sin more. It makes me want to live right and serve. This is not out of obligation, but out of love. This isn't because of who I was, but because of who I am *in Him*.

True transformation begins not with striving, but with belief. When we know and trust that we've already been made free, we stop performing for acceptance and start living from identity—fully alive, fully surrendered, and empowered by grace. This doesn't mean we have no part to play. God doesn't override our will or force us to change. But as we yield to His leading and align our hearts with His truth, grace empowers us to walk out what He's already accomplished in us.

Breaking Free from Religious Expectations

When we begin to measure everything by Scripture, the Holy Spirit gently reveals what needs to stay—and what needs to shift. Letting go of man-made traditions isn't about rebellion; it's about realignment. It's choosing truth over tradition, even when that choice feels uncomfortable. As I began this journey of rediscovery, I noticed that stepping away from certain long-standing traditions sometimes created tension—not necessarily because others meant harm, but because change can feel unsettling when we're used to a certain rhythm.

Before I could look at anyone else, God started with me. He revealed areas of pride in my own heart and reminded me that just because He opened my eyes to something doesn't mean I'm more spiritual than those who may not see it yet. We're all growing—just at different paces. Instead of criticizing, He taught me to pray. Instead of resisting in frustration, He showed me how to gracefully step back from certain activities without carrying offense.

It's not always easy to say no, especially when you're surrounded by people who are genuinely devoted and sincere. I've sat through sermons that seemed to press hard on conformity, and at times that was difficult—but even then, Father reminded me that my freedom in Christ must always be carried with humility. And to this day, He's still teaching me how to walk in that freedom—not with pride, but with grace and love.

Freedom Isn't Lawlessness—It's Spirit-Led Living

Freedom isn't the ability to do whatever we want—it's the power to do what's right without being crushed by shame when we fall short. Grace isn't a license to sin; it's the strength to walk in righteousness. For a long time, I struggled to walk in true freedom because I constantly heard messages about obedience but rarely understood how to bridge the gap between wanting to do what's right and actually doing it. I often felt worn down and defeated, always reminded of where I was falling short. But then I began to see that obedience isn't just about following commands—it's about trusting God and believing His way is better, even when it doesn't make sense.

Obedience Flows from Trust

Obedience flows from trust, not from fear. It's about truly knowing the One who has created us. It's about walking in step with the Spirit, relying on Him to empower us day by day. It's not about striving in our own strength, it's about surrendering to the One who works in us both to will and to do for His good pleasure (Philippians 2:13). I often hear teaching in church that emphasizes human choice. And yes, we absolutely have the ability to choose. But it is the Father who gives us the desire to do His will and empowers us by His Spirit to walk it out. On our own, we can't do anything right—not truly. This isn't an excuse to do nothing or to do wrong; it's an invitation to trust the Father more deeply. It's a call to rest in His power rather than rely on our own.

One of the most frequently emphasized virtues in the life of a born again believer is obedience to God. Churches teach it, Scripture commands it, and we know it's essential. But too often, we present obedience as a stand-alone requirement—something to do simply because "the Bible says so." While this may sound like faithfulness on the surface, it can unintentionally strip obedience of its relational depth.

Obedience is not mechanical. It's not God demanding compliance like a boss issuing orders to subordinates. Instead, obedience is meant to flow from trust. It is a response to the character of a God who is not only holy and powerful but also loving and trustworthy. When we understand who God is—His goodness, His faithfulness, His desire for our flourishing—we begin to see that obedience is not a burden, but a wise response to the One who knows best.

Hebrews 11 gives us a powerful picture of this. The people listed there—Abraham, Moses, Noah, and others—are remembered not just because they obeyed, but because their obedience was born out of trust. They believed God, and their actions followed. Abraham left his homeland because he trusted the promise. Noah built the ark because he trusted God's warning. Trust came first; obedience followed.

This matters deeply for our daily lives. When we teach people to obey without cultivating trust in God, we risk fostering superficial or even resentful compliance. But when we help people encounter God's love and faithfulness, obedience becomes a natural, joyful outworking of that relationship.

In the movie *Clash of the Titans*, the Olympian gods thrived on the worship and fear of mankind—their power rising and falling based on how much people praised or angered them. But the God of the Bible is nothing like that. He isn't a distant or dependent deity who draws strength from human devotion. He doesn't need our obedience to maintain His identity or power. He is already complete—self-sufficient, eternal, and unchanging.

God doesn't call us to obey because He needs affirmation or control. He calls us to obey because *we* need His guidance, protection, and wisdom. Obedience isn't for God's benefit—it's for ours. It's how we walk under the covering of His love, align with His design, and experience the life He created us for. When I truly began to understand, obedience stopped feeling like a burdensome duty. It became a response of trust—my way of saying yes to the God who knows what's best for me and who loves me enough to lead me there.

Freedom Doesn't Mean Chaos

Some people fear that leaving behind religious traditions and rituals will lead to spiritual laziness, moral chaos, or lawlessness. The idea of freedom in Christ is often misunderstood as a license to do whatever we want, with no accountability or guidance. But I've come to understand that true freedom in Christ is nothing like that. It's the most beautiful kind of order—Spirit-led alignment with God's heart and His truth. When the Holy Spirit leads me, He doesn't lead me into confusion or compromise but into truth, holiness, and peace. And He doesn't do it with threats or guilt—He does it with love, by intimacy rather than obligation. It is a freedom born out of a deep relationship with God where I want to honor Him because He loves me, not because I'm trying to avoid punishment. As Scripture reminds us, "Now the Lord is the Spirit, and where the Spirit of the Lord is, there is freedom" (2 Corinthians 3:17). That freedom isn't about doing whatever I want—it's about being free to live fully in His grace and purpose for my life.

This shift began in my mind and heart. Romans 12:2 tells us to "be transformed by the renewing of your mind," and that's exactly what God has been doing in me. Over time, He's helped me unlearn rigid ways of thinking and embrace the freedom found in His grace. Letting go of deeply rooted traditions hasn't always been easy—but for me, it's been essential. Some of those patterns, though well-meaning, created a cycle of striving, performing, and quietly wondering if I was ever truly enough.

Maybe you can relate. Perhaps you were part of a church culture where it felt like doing more somehow meant being more accepted. It's not always something people intentionally teach; sometimes it's simply how we interpret what we've heard or experienced. The beautiful truth is that we don't have to stay in that place. We can allow the Word and the Spirit to reshape our understanding.

You don't always have to reject your past to walk forward in truth. You can honor your roots and still allow God to lead you into deeper relationship. He desires connection over performance and intimacy over obligation. You were created for grace—not to live stuck in rules, but to walk freely in His love and truth. This freedom is your birthright as God's child, and it is available to you today.

Reflection and Response

Ask Yourself:
- How well do I understand the freedom Christ has given me?
- What manmade rules am I holding onto that might be limiting my walk?
- How can trusting God deepen my obedience without feeling like bondage?

A Prayer of Thankfulness for Relationship and Trust

Father,

Thank You for the gift of relationship with You through Christ—not through my works, but through Your grace. I'm so grateful that I don't have to earn Your love or approval. Thank You for teaching me to trust You. That trust is what leads me to obey—not out of fear, but because I know You are faithful and trustworthy.

You always know what's best for me, and I believe You will never lead me astray. I thank You that whatever You ask of me, You have already equipped me to do by Your Spirit. Like the saints of old, I want my trust in You to lead me into joyful obedience—because I know who You are. I love You, Lord.

In Jesus' name, Amen.

Chapter 10: Consistent Communion: Abiding with Father

I checked off my devotion time, meaning I had my scheduled prayer time. I showed up for intercessory prayer and even attended late-night prayer. I felt good when I performed well. I was convinced that if I wasn't present every time a prayer meeting was called, something must be wrong with my relationship with God. I became stuck in a routine of devotion, fitting God into set times instead of inviting Him into every moment of my life. Outside of that routine, I felt distant, but the truth is, I was already distant *because* it had become a routine. The Father never intended our relationship to be about performance or schedules. He didn't save us just to work *through* us, but to be *with* us — walking with us daily in consistent, personal, and loving fellowship.

"Enoch walked faithfully with God…" — *Genesis 5:24 (NIV)*

Before there were priests, temples, or churches… there was a man who simply walked with Father. No title, no public platform, just deep, daily fellowship. And Father was so pleased with him, He took him to heaven.

Father still desires that kind of closeness with His children. Not religious busyness, but intimacy. Not just spiritual discipline but delight in His presence.

Communion Is Consistent Connection

"Abide in me, and I in you… apart from me you can do nothing." John 15:4–5

Communion means abiding. It's not about long prayers or strict routines; it's about continual awareness and ongoing fellowship.

73

You can abide with Father in your car, in the grocery store, while doing household chores, and in conversations, decisions and disappointments. Communion with Father is limitless. He's not waiting for us in a specific room at a specific time. He wants to dwell with us throughout our day. The more we involve Him, the more aware we become of His nearness.

Consistent communion with the Father is about aligning our hearts with His will, not simply presenting our personal requests. The Model Prayer (Matthew 6:9–13; Luke 11:2–4) reminds us to honor God for who He is, submit to His kingdom purposes, and depend on Him for every need. It calls us to forgive freely, stand against evil, and remain steadfast through trials. When our desires yield to His, we begin to see beyond ourselves—becoming sensitive to the needs of the world and advancing His kingdom.

Walking Away from Set Times and Ritual Prayer

If you've ever felt guilty for missing your morning prayer or reading, you're not alone. But guilt isn't Father's motivator—love is. While focused time in the Word and prayer is beneficial, communion isn't confined to a box. Talking to Father is not a task to complete. He's a Person to know. You may have a set time to meet with Him— but don't leave Him there. Walk with Him. Talk to Him. Involve Him. Ask Him about your decisions. Share your emotions. Let Him speak back. Let Him into your *entire* day. That's communion.

I remember learning the five steps of prayer: start with thanksgiving and praise, move into repentance, then intercession for others, followed by supplication for yourself, and finally close with thanksgiving again—thanking God in advance for the answer. For some, this kind of structure can be helpful. It teaches focus, reverence, and intentionality in prayer. But for me, it eventually became more of a formula than a conversation. The routine started to feel so structured and formal that it made me hesitant to talk to God freely. I began to wonder, *why do I have to follow all these steps just to speak with my Father?* I needed real, personal connections.

I remember standing before Him one day, frustrated and complaining about the entire ritual. As clear as day, I heard the Lord say, "I didn't tell you to pray like that." He told me to just talk to Him. So, with a sincere heart, I simply began to talk to my Father. In that instance, I sensed an amazing presence that overwhelmed me and caused me to bow and break into tears. From that day forward, I walked away from that prayer ritual and stepped into real communion—where prayer became a real conversation with my loving Father.

When I was dating my husband, he gave me a small book called *The Practice of the Presence of God.* It took my prayer life with the Father to a deeper level. The book didn't dismiss having set times for prayer, but it opened my eyes to something even more powerful—inviting God into every moment of my day. I began to understand that I didn't have to carve out time for God as if He were separate from the rest of my life. Instead, I became aware of His presence at every moment. That constant communion became far more fulfilling to me than a strict devotional routine.

I'm not criticizing set devotional times—they're helpful, especially for those with structured schedules. In fact, there are times when I do need to sit quietly and intentionally remove distractions to commune with Father. I have my own consistent Bible study. But the freedom of not being bound to a ritual or rigid time frame has been a breath of fresh air. I've discovered that true relationship with God isn't about a routine—it's about walking with Him, moment by moment, in love and awareness.

Consistent Fellowship Brings Consistent Transformation

Consistent fellowship with Father changes you; not just emotionally—but spiritually and practically. You begin to recognize

His voice, respond differently, experience peace in chaos, and sense when He's grieving or leading.

"But we all, with unveiled face… are being transformed into the same image from glory to glory, just as by the Spirit of the Lord." — *2 Corinthians 3:18 (NKJV)*

The more we see Him, the more we become like Him. And you can't see Him clearly without communing with Him consistently. How do you cultivate this communion? Just start talking to Him. Don't come to "do something." Just come to *be*. Let silence be okay. Let your heart settle. Talk to Father honestly. No need for lofty language. Be raw. Be honest. Be real. Invite Him into your day. Keep a listening heart. He speaks through the Word, impressions, peace, and people. Stay connected throughout the day. Whisper prayers. Listen for prompts. Praise Him in the mundane. Acknowledge Him at all times—not just when you need something.

Most of the time, I don't go to God with a list of personal requests. I simply talk to Him as if He's right there in the room with me, like a close friend. I share what's on my mind, ask Him questions, and often pause just to acknowledge how wonderful He is and how thankful I am that He's with me. I pray for others, ask for help when I misplace my keys, and lean on Him when I don't know how to do something. Sometimes, I just talk—no agenda, no structure—just heart-to-heart conversation. And then there are moments when I say nothing at all and simply listen. Mom said I talked a lot when I was younger. I needed to learn to listen. Communing with Father is definitely an opportunity to listen. I count it a privilege to be able to commune with a perfect and holy God. It amazes me that He truly cares about what I think and how I feel. Even when my feelings are off, He loves me enough to guide me in the right direction. There's no better place for me to be than in His presence—anytime, anywhere.

Reflection and Response

Ask Yourself:

- Am I consistently communing with God, or just going through spiritual routines?
- What areas of my life feel disconnected from His presence?
- How is my relationship with God shaping who I'm becoming day by day?

A Prayer of Thankfulness for God's Daily Presence

Father,

Thank You for Your constant presence with me every day. I'm so grateful that I don't have to follow a strict ritual or be in a specific place to talk to You. I can come to You anytime, anywhere, and simply be honest—because I know You care about every part of my life. Thank You for the freedom to walk with You, to share my heart with You, and to commune with You in the small and big moments. Your nearness is such a gift.

In Jesus' name, Amen.

Latonya Sterling

Chapter 11: Fruit That Remains: Living a Life That Honors God Beyond Surface Works

The longer I walk with Father, the more I realize that He isn't impressed by how much I do, how much I know, or how many people applaud. What pleases Him most is that my life bears fruit that remains. Not performance fruit. Not temporary behavior changes. But lasting transformation—character, obedience, humility, and love that flows from intimate relationship with Him. Jesus didn't call us to look spiritual. He called us to be fruitful.

"You did not choose Me, but I chose you and appointed you so that you might go and bear fruit—fruit that will last..." — John 15:16 (NIV)

Father Wants You More Than He Wants Your Work

In Mark 11:12–14, 20–21, Jesus approached a fig tree full of leaves but found no fruit. He cursed it—not because it was visibly broken, but because it was outwardly impressive yet inwardly barren. The tree appeared healthy from a distance, but it had nothing to offer. This was more than a simple act; it was a living parable of spiritual hypocrisy. That fig tree represents many lives today: outwardly spiritual—active in church, fluent in Christian language—but lacking the inner fruit that comes only from a surrendered life. The lesson is sobering. True fruit cannot be faked. It doesn't come from activity, titles, or visibility. It comes from abiding.

"I am the vine; you are the branches. If you remain in me and I in you, you will bear much fruit; apart from me you can do nothing." — John 15:5 (NIV)

The next day, the disciples saw the same fig tree—withered from the roots. This wasn't just about a tree; it pointed to something much deeper: a spiritual reality. Fruitlessness carries weight. When we neglect consistent fellowship with our source—Jesus—even if our lives appear full and vibrant on the outside, we begin to wither internally. It's not about losing salvation, but about losing vitality, joy, and effectiveness in our walk with God.

I've come to realize that Father didn't save me to recruit me into religious activity—He saved me so I could know Him and be loved by Him. From that place of love, I'm able to love others—genuinely, freely, and fruitfully. Intimacy with Him will naturally lead to a desire to serve, but that service flows from relationship, not obligation. It's not about public roles or performance; it's about the overflow of a heart surrendered to Him.

In many church communities, there are wonderful opportunities to get involved—children's ministry, marriage ministry, men and women groups, outreach programs, and more. Some people need these outlets for fellowship, or they wouldn't fellowship. These structures can be life-giving and impactful, especially when people are free to serve in ways that align with how God is leading them. But it's important to remember that service should never feel like a requirement to prove your faith or value. Our identity in Christ isn't based on where we serve, but in who we are as sons and daughters of God.

Some of the most powerful ministry happens outside the four walls of the church—in conversations at work, in how we raise our families, or how we show kindness to strangers. Whether you serve within a ministry or outside of one, what matters most is that your service comes from love and led by the Spirit—not pressure or performance.

Fellow Laborers in Christ: Not Tradition, But Love

The church plays a vital role in building community, but true fellowship is meant to extend beyond Sunday services and midweek gatherings. I remember a season when my pastors paused all church activities—not to limit connection, but because God led them to. That experience reminded me how easy it is to lean on structured events for fellowship, rather than intentionally cultivating it in our daily lives. Real community is not just scheduled—it's shared through everyday moments as we walk with God and with one another.

My husband and I have hosted simple gatherings in our home for years, sometimes focused on Scripture, many times just connecting with people. Even without a formal agenda, those moments often turn into meaningful ministry. What mattered is that the fellowship was honorable to Him. Fellowship doesn't need a microphone or a platform. It flows from a heart that carries God's love wherever it goes.

It's also important to remember that while church activities are valuable and can foster growth, they aren't the only indicators of spiritual maturity. I once watched a movie that portrayed a church filled with nonstop programs and events, yet many of the people weren't reflecting Christ in their daily lives. It reminded me that true transformation isn't measured by a packed church calendar, but by a life that walks with God beyond the building. I'm grateful to be part of a ministry that encourages both fellowship and personal growth—where the focus isn't just on doing for God but being with Him.

Because laypeople sometimes carry expectations, we sometimes forget that pastors carry weight too. Many pastors pour into others tirelessly, often without acknowledgment. They're not looking for thanks—but their time, effort, and sacrifices matter. When people place unfair expectations on them without showing appreciation or stepping up to help, it can be deeply discouraging. Ministry is not a one-sided effort; it's a shared calling. And when we all carry it together, it becomes lighter for everyone.

What Is the Fruit That Remains?

When Jesus spoke in John 15:16, "I chose you and appointed you so that you might go and bear fruit—fruit that will last," He was pointing to the kind of spiritual impact that endures beyond a moment. This fruit includes both inner transformation and the way that transformation shows up in everyday life. The fruit of the Spirit—love, joy, peace, patience, kindness, goodness, faithfulness, gentleness, and self-control—reflects Christ's character being formed in us (Galatians 5:22–23). Joy is choosing gratitude and celebrating God's goodness, even in the middle of a hard season. Peace shows when a believer trusts God instead of panicking during financial uncertainty. Patience is when a mother responds calmly to her child's repeated disobedience, choosing to teach instead of yelling. Kindness might be as simple as smiling and paying for a stranger's coffee without expecting anything in return. Goodness shows when someone refuses to participate in gossip at work and instead speaks truth with integrity. Faithfulness is seen in the spouse who stays committed and prayerful through a difficult marriage. Gentleness is shown when correcting someone who is wrong, not with harsh words but with humility and compassion. And self-control is practiced when you walk away from temptation— even if it means deleting a social media app or refusing to watch something everyone else is talking about. These are all expressions of the kind of fruit that remains. And beyond our personal growth, this fruit impacts others—when we share the gospel, disciple a new believer, or offer godly counsel that leads someone closer to Christ. These aren't just momentary actions; they leave a spiritual legacy. God didn't just call us to experience Him occasionally—He chose us to live in such a way that His presence is consistently revealed through us, producing fruit that endures for eternity.

One of the most unmistakable signs of God's presence in a believer's life is a genuine love for others, especially when loving them costs us something. Jesus said that this kind of love is how the world would recognize His followers. It isn't selective, shallow, or self-serving—it reflects the sacrificial heart of Christ.

Because God is love, love must be at the core of who we are as His people. Everything we do should flow from that love—not from fear, duty, or pride. The church in Ephesus (Revelation 2:1–7) offers a sobering reminder. Though they were praised for their hard work, perseverance, and moral discernment, Jesus confronted them for abandoning the deep, devoted love they once had for Him. Their passion had faded, and without love, even their good works lost their power. That early devotion—their "first love"—had once fueled their obedience and joy. Without it, they risked losing their spiritual influence altogether. Jesus warned that if they didn't return to that love, their lampstand—their light, authority, and presence—would be removed. He wasn't speaking of lost salvation, but of a loss of effectiveness and impact as His representatives.

These warnings still echo today. As individuals and churches, we must guard against doing the right things for wrong reasons. Activity without love is just noise. True fruit is the visible evidence of God's Spirit working in us—it's not about perfection but about transformation. When our lives remain rooted in Christ, our fruit endures, reflects His heart, and draws others to Him.

I strongly believe in living a life that honors God—not just privately, but publicly as well. Still, we must be careful not to confuse personal convictions with biblical commands. Sometimes, in our zeal, we impose our own standards on others—judging their spirituality based on how they speak, dress, or behave. When others don't meet our expectations, it's easy to become critical without realizing it.

Many quote the phrase, "You can tell a tree by the fruit it bears," as a way to evaluate someone else's spiritual state. But when Jesus spoke those words, He was warning against false prophets—those who appear godly on the outside but have corrupt hearts (Matthew 7:15–20). The "fruit" in that passage refers to consistent patterns of character and influence, not isolated failures or moments of weakness.

So, if a believer stumbles, speaks harshly, or even loses their temper—does that mean they've lost their salvation? Absolutely not. Salvation is the work of God's grace, and that grace is still at work in all of us. The fruit Jesus described isn't a checklist to judge others, but an invitation to examine ourselves. Are we growing in love, patience, humility, and truth? Is our character continuously being shaped by the Spirit?

The kind of fruit God desires is not flashy or superficial. It's the kind that grows in hidden places, through quiet surrender and consistent fellowship with Him. It reflects not just behavior, but a transformed heart.

Ultimately, honoring God isn't about appearances or performance—it's about authenticity. Outward fruit can be a sign of spiritual growth, but real change begins in the heart. Instead of focusing on the branches of someone else's life, we should allow God to cultivate fruit in our own lives, fruit that remains, fruit that glorifies Him, and fruit that draws others to His love.

Reflection and Response

Ask Yourself:

- Am I more focused on doing for God than becoming like Him?
- Is the fruit of the Spirit visible in my everyday relationships and choices?
- Do I allow the Holy Spirit to shape my character, or am I trying to manage behavior on my own?

Prayer to Know and Serve God Freely

Father,

I come to You with a sincere heart, desiring to know You more. I want to understand who You are beyond rules, titles, or expectations. Teach me to walk closely with You, to hear Your voice, and to be led by Your Spirit in every area of my life. Help me to serve where You want me to serve—not out of obligation, guilt, or pressure from man, but from a heart that loves and honors You. I don't want to be bound by religious requirements that make me feel like I'm not enough if I'm not serving in a church ministry. Thank You, Father, that You don't see me that way.

You know my heart. You know how I long to please You—not for man's approval, but for Your glory. Thank You for reminding me that my obedience to You is what matters most. Lead me in paths of righteousness for Your name's sake.

In Jesus' name, Amen.

Latonya Sterling

Chapter 12: The Beauty of Fellowship

On October 3, 1993, I turned back to Christ after being backslidden for eleven years. What I didn't anticipate was the expectation of going to church every single Sunday. I still remember one Sunday when Duane showed up at my house. I came to the door wearing my robe and a satin cap on my head. He asked, "Why didn't you go to church?" I replied, "I'm supposed to go every Sunday?" His answer was a simple, "Yes." From that point on, I committed to attending church every Sunday and Bible study every Wednesday night.

I enjoyed it. I learned a lot. The praise and worship was incredible—Christ-centered music at its best. I became involved in the children's ministry and discovered how much I enjoyed teaching. Eventually, I was placed in leadership and later began training youth for leadership. I loved my church family. I had amazing mentors and mature sisters in Christ. Church life felt perfect.

But as the years went by, I began to feel like something was missing. In my pursuit of understanding what that "something" was, I discovered that attending church every Sunday and midweek Bible study weren't biblical commands. The more I learned, the more I realized that I believed things that kept me tethered to church routines rather than rooted in the liberty of Christ. Still, the fear of what others might think if I broke the routine kept me stuck in a religious cycle for years. Going to church became a chore.

Eventually, my husband and I became part of another ministry, where we stayed for about six years. It was a beautiful community, led by loving pastors. I oversaw the children's ministry, and we served in the marriage ministry. It was a blessing to our own marriage and spiritual growth. But over time, I began to feel that same weariness with the routine creeping in again.

We eventually transitioned to another ministry, not knowing what God had in store. In the beginning, it was wonderful. The pastors were genuinely loving people with servant hearts. But once the novelty wore off, I started seeing some of the same traditional patterns I had been trying to escape. I was ready to leave. I had never actually heard God tell me to go to nor leave a ministry as I have heard other people profess. I simply exercised my freedom to fellowship with believers where I wanted to fellowship. But this time, God spoke. Instead, He gently told me to stay. I wanted to leave several times, but every time I had the inclination to leave, God said, "Stay." And with each act of obedience, a layer of pride, offense, or misconception fell off me. I began to appreciate the people. I stopped being critical of the messages. I started to see my pastors' hearts even more beyond the things I didn't fully agree with. Slowly but surely, I began to genuinely love my church family. I got to the point where I missed them when I wasn't around them.

So how did I get there? By staying when I wanted to run. By listening when I wanted to tune out. And by letting God do the deep work in me that I never knew I needed.

While our relationship with Father is personal, it's not life on an island. While I really dislike what I call "institutionalized church," Father showed me the beauty and necessity of fellowship with other believers.

The Need for Fellowship

While the Bible doesn't command us to attend church every Sunday or midweek gathering, it does emphasize the importance of fellowship among believers. Psalm 133:1 says, "Behold, how good and pleasant it is when brothers dwell in unity." The unity David describes is rooted in Israel's relationship with God and expressed in their relationship with one another. As believers, we need each other—whether we're new to the faith or seasoned in it. Isolation can leave us vulnerable, and some especially need the strength that comes from being covered, encouraged, and sharpened by the body of Christ.

Sadly, in some church environments, spiritual maturity has been equated with church attendance, and believers have felt pressure to conform out of guilt or fear. But not all pastors are trying to manipulate or control. In fact, many carry a deep, God-given burden to see God's people grow, flourish, and experience His love in tangible ways. Their desire to see consistent fellowship often stems from care, not condemnation.

Still, even sincere leadership can unintentionally place heavy expectations on others. Jesus never led with pressure—He led with truth and compassion. True shepherds lead by example, not guilt. Real fellowship is a gift from God, not a religious requirement. The goal isn't to abandon the gathering of believers, but to free it from man-made pressure and return it to what God intended—an authentic, life-giving expression of love, growth, and community in Christ.

Sometimes Hebrews 10:25 is used to pressure people to come to church. The message in Hebrews 10:25 wasn't about forcing people to attend church services. At the time, Jewish believers were under intense persecution under Nero's rule. In an attempt to avoid torture and death, many were tempted to return to the safety of the synagogues—places that had rejected Jesus as the Messiah. The writer of Hebrews was urging them not to return to the old Judean system but to continue fellowshipping with fellow believers in Christ. These believers weren't rejecting fellowship altogether—they were choosing to gather with people who did not share their faith in Jesus, and that was the danger.

As believers, it is vital that we stay connected to a community of like-minded people. Even with my issues, I could hear Father speak. Listening to Father kept me grounded in a place where I could grow spiritually. Being part of a local community of believers means having real friends—people who care about you, who will pray for you, who love you enough to correct you when needed. You're not just part of a congregation; you're part of a family.

Today, I no longer attend church out of religious obligation or guilt. I go because I genuinely love being with my Kingdom family and value the opportunity to grow with others in Christ. I've also come to appreciate that believers can worship in different places and expressions—and I celebrate the diversity in the Body of Christ. I have dear brothers and sisters who attend other church communities, and I honor the work God is doing through them too.

There are times I may not attend a service or function, and I've learned to walk in peace about that. I'm grateful that the ministry I attend encourages spiritual growth without placing pressure to be at every event. I've come to seek the Lord's direction in how I show up— and He's always faithful to lead. When He prompts me to serve or participate, I do so with joy. Sometimes, I choose to be present simply out of love for the people God has placed in my life.

At the same time, I've come to appreciate the heart and labor of our pastors. Their time, preparation, and spiritual care are not small things. It blesses them when the people they pour into show up with willing hearts. Even when pastors don't seek recognition, it matters when we follow through on commitments and respond to their efforts with support. Pastors can become weary too, especially when people casually disengage after verbally committing. I've learned that honoring them isn't about pressure, it's about love, maturity, and shared responsibility in the body.

That's the difference for me now: I no longer move from guilt or obligation, but from love—both for God and for His people. Christ has given me freedom, and in that freedom, I've found joy in showing up with purpose. I'm still growing in this—learning how to walk it out with humility, gratitude, and a heart that values both liberty and leadership.

This journey into freedom also changed how I parent. Early on, I made my daughters attend church out of religious obligation, assuming it would help them love God more. But instead, it became a routine—not a relationship. When our sons were young, they came because they had to, but as they got older, I noticed their disinterest. They weren't connecting to what was being taught, and I didn't want to risk them resenting God because I was forcing something that felt empty. It troubled me greatly, and I didn't know what to do. When I brought this to the Lord, He gently reminded me: "Don't force them—just teach them." That shifted everything. Father reminded me that it wasn't the church's job to disciple our kids—it was ours. So, we made Bible study a greater priority at home. And once I stopped making church a requirement, something amazing happened—our sons began choosing spiritual environments for themselves. Of course we had to approve. They started attending youth group at the church community attached to their Christian school, where they were already immersed in regular Bible teaching and chapel.

At first, I worried about what others would think when we came to church without our kids. But we chose to follow God's lead for our family. We never had to declare, "As for me and my house ...," because our focus was to live it—not force it. We lead by example, stay consistent in our walk, and give our kids access to truth and community, trusting God to draw their hearts.

Seek God for what's best for your family. His path for you may look different than ours—but He will lead you well.

The Blessing of Fellowship

Fellowship with other believers is not just a good idea, it's a helpful part of our spiritual growth. While our relationship with the Father is deeply personal, spiritual maturity often happens in community. God uses others to sharpen us, challenge us, and help us apply the truths we've learned in real-life situations. True fellowship allows us to practice grace, forgiveness, patience, and love in a tangible way. It also creates space for the gifts God has placed in each of us to be activated and used to build up the Body. When we gather in unity, we reflect the very nature of God, who Himself exists in perfect fellowship—Father, Son, and Holy Spirit. There's something sacred to me about being surrounded by people who love Jesus and love you. That kind of connection not only strengthens your walk, it protects you from the dangers of isolation. The enemy loves to work in silence and secrecy, but fellowship keeps us seen, supported, and spiritually grounded. Beyond enjoying my Kingdom family, I now understand that fellowship is a vital part of my growth. In community, I'm reminded that I'm not alone, that my gifts matter, and that God designed us to walk this journey together—not out of obligation, but out of shared purpose, encouragement, and love.

Reflection and Response

Ask Yourself:
- Do I see fellowship as a gift from God or a religious duty?
- Am I intentionally building relationships that encourage my spiritual growth?
- When I gather with believers, is it out of love and desire, or out of pressure and obligation?

Prayer of Gratitude for Fellowship and Freedom

Father,

I thank You for opening my eyes to the true value of fellowship. Thank You for setting me free from the religious pressure to attend church out of guilt or obligation. Instead, You've shown me the beauty of gathering with Your people—not because I have to, but because I get to. Thank You for surrounding me with brothers and sisters in Christ who help me grow, challenge me in love, and walk alongside me on this journey of faith. Thank You for the opportunity to walk in love, to practice grace, and to build meaningful relationships rooted in You. I'm grateful for the spiritual family You've given me and the freedom to follow Your Spirit without fear or shame. Help me to continue cherishing fellowship, not as a requirement, but as a gift. In Jesus' name, Amen.

Latonya Sterling

Chapter 13: Freedom in Giving: A Heart Transformed by Truth

One of the things I learned early in church was the practice of giving. This wasn't something that bothered me. In fact, it felt good when the pastor preached about tithing and I knew I was among those who gave faithfully. When I started attending church regularly in 1993, giving came naturally. As a single woman, I was constantly helping people financially. I didn't make a lot of money, but if I had it to give, I would give it many times without hesitation or questions. I had been taught that tithing and giving were biblical commands, and I genuinely wanted to honor God. So, no matter what my income was, He got a tenth.

When I met my husband, he was also a tither. So, when we married, there was no battle—giving a tenth was something we both were accustomed to. Over time, we heard many messages about giving, often rooted in promises of blessing or warnings of loss. I remember one pastor saying, "If you have a need, show God your checkbook and remind Him of how many times you wrote your tithe check"—as if our giving gave us leverage with God.

I also think about the building fund we sowed into faithfully. In the end, the building was still incomplete, and the debt remained. That experience changed us. We agreed that moving forward, we wouldn't commit to another building fund unless God clearly led us to do so. It wasn't because we didn't want to give—we absolutely believe in generosity—but we also believe that when God truly ordains something, He moves on the hearts of His people to give freely, not under pressure. In Exodus 36:5–7, the people gave so much for the tabernacle that Moses had to stop them—they were giving in response to God, not guilt. So, if God moves upon your heart to sow into a building fund, by all means, give joyfully. For us, that kind of giving must come from His prompting, not pressure. Later, we came into a large sum of money. Out of habit, we gave a tenth to the church. But shortly after, we encountered a sister in Christ with a real need, and we couldn't help her because we'd already given the money to the church. That moment lit a fire in my soul. Wait a minute, I thought. If there's a brother or sister in Christ in need, then helping them is also giving to God. I'll discuss New Testament giving later in this chapter.

What Is a Tithe, Biblically?

The word tithe simply means "a tenth." It was originally part of the Mosaic Law given to the Israelites—not the Gentiles. God instructed the people of Israel to give a tenth of their agricultural increase as an act of worship and obedience (Leviticus 27:30–32, Numbers 18:21–24). These tithes supported the Levites (the priestly tribes who had no land of their own), the temple, and those in need, including orphans and widows.

The tithe wasn't just one offering—it was part of a broader system of giving, which when added up, was closer to 20–23% annually. But here's the key: this was a command to the people of Israel under the Old Covenant, not to the Gentile church under grace.

Abraham and Melchizedek: A Voluntary Gift

Some teachings on tithing point to Abraham's interaction with Melchizedek (Genesis 14:18–20) as a pre-law example to support tithing in the New Covenant church. After rescuing Lot and winning a battle, Abraham gave Melchizedek—a priest and king—a tenth of the spoils of war. But this was not a command from God; it was a one-time, voluntary act of honor and thanksgiving. In fact, Abraham later stated he didn't want anyone to say they made him rich except God (Genesis 14:23). This moment was about worship and trust—not obligation. The book of Hebrews later references this event, but not to mandate tithing for New Testament believers. Instead, the writer uses Melchizedek to demonstrate the superiority of Jesus Christ's priesthood. Addressing Jewish believers tempted to return to the old Levitical system, Hebrews highlights that Jesus, like Melchizedek, is both King and Priest—not by lineage or law, but by divine appointment. Abraham's gift acknowledged Melchizedek's spiritual authority, just as we now honor Christ as our eternal High Priest. Hebrews 7:12 underscores this shift: "For when the priesthood is changed, the law must be changed also." The reference to tithing is therefore not an instruction, but a theological comparison. Under the New Covenant, we are no longer bound by the legal system that required tithes. Our giving now flows from grace, not law—from relationship, not obligation.

Understanding the Context of Malachi

Malachi 3:8–10—"Will a man rob God?"—is one of the most quoted Scriptures when it comes to tithing. Many of us have heard it used to emphasize the importance of giving. But to truly honor God's Word, we must understand its original context. Malachi's message was directed not to the New Testament church, but to the priests of Israel who were dishonoring God with corrupt sacrifices and failing to care for the people as the Law required. The tithes they withheld were part of the Old Covenant system that supported the temple, the Levites, and the poor.

For believers under the New Covenant, our relationship with God is no longer governed by the Mosaic Law but shaped by grace and faith in Christ. The blessings of God aren't earned through external obedience to rules but received through surrendered hearts that walk in wisdom and trust. Galatians 5:18 says, "But if you are led by the Spirit, you are not under the law." This means we are not bound to obey Mosaic Law for righteousness. We are not under that system of legalism or performance.

Some believers testify that their finances improved when they began tithing, and that may be true. But the fruit they experienced likely came not from following a formula, but from placing their trust in God for provision and help in governing their finances. This leads to better financial stewardship. When we honor God with what we have, not from compulsion but from love and trust, we invite His wisdom and provision into our lives.

Giving in the New Testament

When you get to the New Testament, the emphasis around giving shifts. There's no direct command for believers in Christ to tithe, but we are clearly called to give—cheerfully, generously, sacrificially, and willingly. As 2 Corinthians 9:7 says, "God loves a cheerful giver," and in verse 6, "Whoever sows sparingly will also reap sparingly." The early church shared their possessions to meet the needs of others (Acts 2:44–45), and giving was always a matter of the heart: "Each of you should give what you have decided in your heart to give" (2 Corinthians 9:7). Giving isn't a transaction to get something from God—it's about love, freedom from materialism, and a willingness to meet real needs. As 1 John 3:17 reminds us, if we see a brother or sister in need and have no compassion, how can the love of God be in us?

Sowing faithfully into a ministry is good because practical things cost. Many pastors—like the ones who lead the ministry I attend—work regular jobs and take nothing from the church. I've watched them personally cover needs without making a show or demanding anything in return. They don't guilt or pressure us to give, and yet they give freely. Still, it's important to recognize that Scripture supports caring for those who minister the gospel. "The Lord has commanded that those who preach the gospel should receive their living from the gospel" (1 Corinthians 9:14). When we withhold honor and support from those who pour themselves out spiritually, we miss an opportunity to partner in what God is doing through them.

98

Still, there are people who regularly benefit from the ministry's resources and never sow into it. That doesn't stop our pastors—or likely others, from helping where help is needed. At the same time, it's completely understandable if someone cannot give financially, especially if they're between jobs or facing hardship. God sees the heart. But if you are part of a ministry and *can* give, sow into what is necessary for that ministry to function. After all, you should consider the ministry you attend family. It honors God when we help one another. It simply doesn't make sense to sit in a place and never see the value in sowing into it, especially when you're able to do so.

Living Proof of God's Faithfulness

My husband and I have never gone without. We've never had to borrow to meet our household needs. And while we don't tithe in the traditional sense, we give—generously, joyfully, and purposefully. We give to our church and to those in need, and time and again, we've seen God move in unexpected ways to meet our needs. We haven't always made perfect financial choices—we've made our share of mistakes—but God has always been faithful, and we don't take His favor for granted.

What gave validity to our changed perspective on giving was understanding through the lens of the New Testament. Instead of treating it like a rule to follow, we began to see giving as a response to God's love. That shift didn't make us give less—it stirred us to give more. Heart-led generosity has deepened our desire to sow sacrificially and intentionally. We're committed to helping others outside the church, but we also make sure to give consistently to our place of fellowship. We understand the practical needs of ministry and deeply honor the continual outpouring of our pastors. Our giving isn't driven by obligation, but by gratitude—for God, for His people, and for the spiritual home He's entrusted to us.

Honestly, I can't imagine being part of a ministry for years, having money in my pocket, and not seeing the value in sowing into it. If I go to a movie, I pay for a ticket. If I eat at a restaurant, I pay for a meal. I'm not giving in church to get something in return—but when I see a ministry walking in purpose and integrity, the least I can do is support what God is doing through it. Ministries require resources to function, and giving becomes an honor—not a burden—when it flows from love and alignment with God's heart.

Giving Beyond Money: Time and Talents

The greatest lesson I've learned is that giving isn't just about money. It's about giving our time, talents, and heart. In Matthew 25:14–30, Jesus tells a parable about a master who entrusts three servants with different amounts of money (called "talents"). Two of the servants invest what they were given and double it. The third, out of fear, hides his and returns only what he was given. The master praises the first two, calling them "faithful," but rebukes the third. The message? We're expected to use what God gives us—whether money, skills, or opportunities—for His glory.

Final Thoughts

As you grow in your understanding of God's heart, take time to study what the Bible teaches about tithes and offerings. Don't give out of fear, pressure, religious obligation, or hope of getting something in return. Instead, give out of freedom and joy. God gave His only begotten Son out of love. So, let your giving be a response to that undeserved love.

If giving has been a struggle for you in the church—if it's ever felt like a burden or manipulation, ask God to show you what it means to be a cheerful, Spirit-led giver. You may find the freedom, joy, and fruitfulness you've been missing.

Reflection and Response

Ask Yourself:
- Am I giving cheerfully and intentionally, or out of routine and pressure?
- Do I see giving as a partnership with God and my local ministry, sowing where I'm spiritually fed?
- How can I be more faithful in giving not just my finances, but also my time and talents for God's glory?

Latonya Sterling

Prayer: A Heart to Give

Father,

Thank You for being the ultimate Giver. You gave Your only Son so that I could have eternal life, and You continue to provide everything I need day by day. Lord, I ask that You help me to be a faithful and wise steward of all You've entrusted to me—my finances, my time, my gifts, and my heart.

Produce in me a generous spirit, one that is eager to help others, especially those with genuine needs. Even when I don't have much to give, remind me that even my prayers are a gift when offered in love and faith. Teach me to give not out of guilt or pressure, but out of gratitude and grace.

Help me to understand what it truly means to give biblically—led by Your Spirit and rooted in love. Show me how to offer not just my money, but my time and talents for Your glory. Help me to be a vessel You can use, always ready to serve, share, and bless.

Father, remove every trace of stinginess from my heart. Free me from giving to earn something in return, to gain approval, or out of fear. Instead, help me to give joyfully, sincerely, and sacrificially, trusting that You are my source and that You see and honor what is done in secret.

Shape my heart to reflect Yours—a heart that delights in giving.

In Jesus' name, Amen.

Chapter 14: Walking in Truth: Discernment in an Age of Deception

I didn't grow up in church, but I've been walking with the Lord and serving in ministry for over 30 years. Along the way, I've received teachings that were deeply transformative—and others that were more rooted in tradition than truth. I've only been part of three ministries during my journey, and in each one, I was blessed to serve under the leadership of pastors who were sincere, loving, and committed to honoring God.

Yet even in these rich spiritual environments, I began to realize how easily tradition can find its way into the life of the church. It surprised me to discover that deeply held teachings—shared by people who genuinely love the Lord and study His Word—could sometimes be based more on longstanding customs than on New Covenant truth. When I began to experience freedom in certain areas, I didn't always respond well. At times, I grew frustrated and even critical. Rather than praying for my leaders, I judged them—grieving over the years I'd unknowingly lived in spiritual bondage.

But God, in His grace, gently corrected my heart. He helped me see that my leaders weren't trying to mislead or burden anyone. They were simply sharing what they believed to be true, seeking to please God with pure hearts and faithful service. That realization humbled me and taught me to respond with compassion rather than criticism.

Over the years, I've witnessed growth not only in myself but also in the body of Christ. I've seen pastors courageously acknowledge and revise certain teachings. I've watched as traditions gave way to greater revelation and clarity. Still, I know there are many believers who remain caught in a mixture of Old and New Covenant thinking—not out of rebellion, but because these doctrines have been passed down over generations.

This is why God continues to work on my heart—not just in doctrine, but in attitude. He's teaching me to pray instead of judge, to intercede for others the same way I needed intercession when I was still unlearning and relearning. It's not easy to surrender deeply held beliefs or to admit that we may have misunderstood Scripture. But humility is the path to deeper truth.

As 2 Timothy 2:24–25 reminds us, "The Lord's servant must not be quarrelsome but must be kind to everyone, able to teach, not resentful. Opponents must be gently instructed, in the hope that God will grant them repentance leading them to a knowledge of the truth." And John 16:13 assures us that only the Holy Spirit can lead us into all truth. That truth comforts me. It frees me from trying to change others and reminds me to stay surrendered to God's refining work in my own heart.

The process of transformation is different for everyone. Our responsibility isn't to manage someone else's journey, but to continue being transformed ourselves—"from glory to glory into the image of Christ" (2 Corinthians 3:18). When we walk in truth with humility and grace, we don't just stop bad teaching, we embody the heart of the Father, offering others a safe place to learn, grow, and discover Him more deeply.

Being Anchored in the Safety of Truth

As I continued to grow in my relationship with the Father, I noticed something that stirred a deep awareness in me—there were so many voices, all claiming to speak on His behalf. From pulpits to podcasts, books to social media posts, my heart was being pulled in countless directions. While some messages inspired and edified me, others left me feeling confused, unsettled, or spiritually drained. That's when I began asking a vital question: *How do I know what's truly from God?*

In today's spiritually noisy world, that question isn't just about gaining knowledge, it's about staying spiritually anchored. Scripture warns us that not everything labeled "spiritual" is from God: "Dear friends, do not believe every spirit, but test the spirits to see whether they are from God" (1 John 4:1). Discernment isn't optional; it's essential. Deception doesn't always come wrapped in obvious error—it often comes dressed in charisma, coated with Scripture, and presented with sincerity.

But I've come to realize that truth is more than sound doctrine, it's a person. Jesus said, "I am the way and the truth and the life" (John 14:6). The more I focused on Jesus Himself, the clearer things became. If a message pulls me away from Christ, distorts the heart of God, or contradicts Scripture in context—even if it sounds convincing—it's not truth. I've learned that the safest place I can be is anchored in Him, with the Word of God as my foundation and the Holy Spirit as my guide.

Thankfully, we aren't left to navigate this alone. "When the Spirit of truth comes, He will guide you into all the truth" (John 16:13). That's a promise. The Holy Spirit gently alerts us when something isn't right—even before we can articulate why. I've learned to pause and ask, "Holy Spirit, is this from You?" He's always faithful to respond. But I also had a part to play: I had to know God's Word for myself. It's easy to rely on others for spiritual insight, but secondhand revelation cannot sustain us in a world full of counterfeit truth. "Your word is a lamp to my feet and a light to my path" (Psalm 119:105). The more familiar I became with Scripture, the more easily I recognized when something didn't line up.

We also have to guard our hearts against the tendency to chase what feels good rather than what is true. As Paul wrote, "The time will come when people will not put up with sound doctrine... but will gather around them a great number of teachers to say what their itching ears want to hear" (2 Timothy 4:3). It's not about judging anyone's intentions—it's about remaining anchored in truth when trends, emotions, or culture try to sway us.

Discernment, I've learned, functions like a spiritual immune system. It doesn't just protect us from false doctrine; it keeps our hearts tender, our minds clear, and our faith rooted in Christ. For me, that has meant limiting my intake of spiritual voices to those who teach sound doctrine and live with humility and fruit. It's also meant staying planted in a Spirit-led community, where iron sharpens iron and truth is spoken in love.

In a world filled with noise, I'm learning to quiet my soul, sit with the Father, and listen for His voice above all others. He's always speaking. He speaks to me through His Word and through a sense of peace. He will lead me to someone of wisdom. Sometimes I may have a since of uncertainty that makes me stop. Many times, that's a warning for me to stand still or stand down. And when I stay close, I stay anchored—safe, steady, and deeply rooted in the truth that sets us free.

Reflection and Response

Ask Yourself:
- Am I anchored in the Word of God, or am I easily swayed by popular teachings and opinions?
- How can I stay humble and teach truth with love, without becoming quarrelsome or prideful?
- Am I guarding my heart against deception by daily seeking the Holy Spirit's guidance and discernment?

Prayer for Discernment, Truth, and Compassion

Father,

Thank You for patiently walking with me as You strip away every wrong doctrine I once held as truth. Thank You for the light of Your Word and the guidance of Your Spirit that continues to expose traditions and teachings that have kept me bound. You are faithful to lead me out of confusion and into clarity—not to shame me, but to set me free. I'm so grateful that You didn't leave me where I was, and that You are still renewing my mind, layer by layer.

Lord, continue to give me discernment—sharpen my spirit to recognize what is from You and what is not. Anchor me in Your truth so I won't be swayed by popularity, emotion, or tradition. Help me to know Your Word deeply, not just so I can recognize error, but so I can walk in the fullness of the freedom You died to give me.

And Father, give me a heart of compassion for those who are still bound by religious traditions or false teachings. Remind me that I was once there too. Help me not to criticize or grow impatient with my leaders or others who teach the Word. Instead, teach me to intercede—to pray for their eyes to be opened, for their hearts to be softened, and for their teaching to be purified by Your Spirit. Help me to walk in love, not pride. Help me to carry truth with humility and grace.

May my life reflect Your character—not just in what I know, but in how I treat others who are still growing. And may everything I speak, teach, and live bring glory to You and point people to Jesus—the Way, the Truth, and the Life.

In Jesus' name I pray, Amen.

Chapter 15: Finishing Well: Enduring to the End with Joy and Faithfulness

Following Jesus is not a sprint—it's a lifelong race of endurance, faith, and obedience. For years, I was running in circles, bound by my religious rituals, checking boxes, and trying to earn what had already been given to me through Christ. But now I understand finishing well is not about religious performance—it's about remaining anchored in Jesus, led by His Spirit, and faithful to His voice. It's not about how often I attend church or how many ministries I lead. It's about whether I trust God through every season, whether I die to my flesh to follow the truth, and whether I keep chasing after Him. The race isn't easy. There are moments of silence, temptation, discouragement, and isolation. But when your eyes are fixed on Jesus—not on applause, routine, or approval—you find strength to endure. I no longer measure my faith by church calendars or external validation. I measure it by love, obedience, and freedom in Christ. I want to finish this race not burned out or bitter, but with joy, peace, and a heart still in love with God. I want to hear Him say, "Well done, good and faithful servant." That's the reward that matters most.

Let Us Finish Well

As I seek to finish well, one of my greatest desires is to teach the Word of God in its proper context—so that people can truly get to know Him. *"They perish for lack of knowledge" (Hosea 4:6)*, and it is my heart's cry that no one would be held captive by misunderstanding or tradition. I want believers to see who they already are in Christ and what they already possess through Him, so they no longer feel the pressure to earn what has freely been given. *"His divine power has given us everything we need for life and godliness through our knowledge of Him" (2 Peter*

109

1:3). There is real freedom in Christ. *"It is for freedom that Christ has set us free. Stand firm, then, and do not let yourselves be burdened again by a yoke of slavery" (Galatians 5:1).*

Because Jesus lives in me, I get to carry His light into the world. Not because I've done everything right or have it all together, but simply because He's with me. His light shines through me—not based on how well I perform, but because He chose to live in me when I gave Him my yes. I don't have to earn His love, and I'm not working my way into heaven. I've been saved by His grace, not by anything I've done. The good things I do now—loving others, making better choices, being kind or forgiving—those aren't ways to prove I'm worthy. They're just the natural result of walking with Him.

I've come to realize that obeying God isn't about fear or pressure. It's about trust. I follow Him because I believe He loves me, He's faithful, and He really does know what's best for my life. That changes everything. It makes following Him feel less like a duty and more like joy. Only He could have renewed my mind in this way.

Take a moment to let this sink in: you can have a real, personal relationship with a perfect God. Not a distant, formal one—but a close, honest, everyday relationship. That might feel hard to believe, especially if you've grown up thinking God was angry, disappointed, or hard to reach. But He's not. He's near, and He wants you to know Him—not just know about Him.

If you've accepted Jesus, His Spirit now lives in you. That means you're never alone. You don't have to try to figure everything out by yourself or clean yourself up to come close to Him. You're already His. And even when you mess up—and we all do—He doesn't walk away. He stays. He helps you get back up every single time.

God's not sitting in heaven waiting to punish you or guilt you into being better. His heart isn't focused on catching you in failure, but on nurturing a deeper, more intimate walk with Him. Yet, because He loves you, there are times He will discipline—just like a loving parent corrects a child—not to condemn, but to guide you back to what brings life. His kindness, His patience, and His unfailing love are what lead you to true change and repentance (Romans 2:4). That's how He works. He's not after outward perfection; He's after an intimate connection that transforms you from the inside out. Grace doesn't erase responsibility—it empowers it. His love invites you to live differently, not by fear of punishment, but by the freedom that comes from being deeply known and loved by Him.

As you spend time with Him and begin to let go of some of the old ways of thinking—whether that's shame from your past or even religious habits that made you feel stuck—your mind and heart will start to change. You'll start to see Him more clearly. You'll begin to experience real freedom. Not just from obvious sin, but from anything that's held you back from truly knowing Him. So, breathe. Relax. Let yourself be free. You are loved, you are being led, and God is not finished with you. Not even close. Draw near to Him and He will draw near to you (James 4:8).

Reflection and Response

Ask Yourself:
- Am I staying faithful to God's leading, even in seasons that feel long or challenging?
- Is my service to God flowing from a heart of love and trust, or from pressure and performance?
- How can I finish well, keeping joy and endurance as I walk out my purpose in Christ?

Latonya Sterling

Closing **Prayer for Deeper Relationship** **and Freedom for All of Us**

Thank You, Father, for being a God who desires to be known—not merely obeyed from a distance but intimately walked with in truth and grace. You have not called us to manmade rules, but to a relationship. You have not given us rules to enslave us, but Your Spirit to lead us into all truth.

Lord, I pray—for myself and for every person reading these words—that You would open the eyes of our hearts to truly know You, not just through tradition or teaching, but through deep, personal revelation. Break every chain of false doctrine, every burden of religious pressure, and every lie that has kept us from seeing You as You truly are—gracious, faithful, kind, and loving.

Help us know, deep in our souls, that we are already accepted, already loved, already chosen in Christ Jesus. Cause Your truth to dismantle every yoke of performance, every shadow of shame, and every weight of guilt. Let the truth of our identity in You take root in our hearts and bear lasting fruit in our lives—fruit that remains. Teach us to walk in the freedom You died to give—to live from Your approval rather than striving for man's. Holy Spirit, lead us into a deeper knowledge of the Father, and show us what it means to walk in the light—not as slaves, but as sons and daughters.

Help us to reflect the beauty of Your workmanship, created in Christ Jesus for good works—not to earn salvation, but as the overflow of hearts that love and trust You. And when we stumble, remind us that You are not finished with us. You are faithful to complete the work You began.

I bless us, Lord, in the name of Yeshua, the Son of the living God. Help us walk in truth. Help us walk in freedom. Help us walk in love.

In Jesus' name,
Amen.

Conclusion: I Trapped Myself

Looking back, I realize that no one tied me to the rituals. No one chained me to the performance. I did that to myself. As a teenager, I didn't know any better. I didn't have anyone walking alongside me to explain grace or identity in Christ. I was just trying to please God the only way I knew how—with good intentions, but no real understanding. And at that stage, I can say I didn't have the tools or maturity to know what I didn't know.

I'm no longer a child. And when I became an adult, I had access to the same God, the same Word, and the same Holy Spirit as anyone else. I can't blame any pastor, leader, or church for the season I stayed stuck in religious cycles. The truth is, I had a Bible. I had the Spirit of God living in me. But instead of pressing in, I chose the easier road—I followed the teachings of others without testing them for myself. I became lazy, and somewhere along the way, I made their voices louder than His.

Let me be clear: I don't believe the church communities I was a part of were manipulative. I don't believe the pastors were out to control or mislead anyone. They taught what they genuinely believed. They love God deeply and want people to live holy and pleasing lives before Him. I would die on the hill that their hearts are pure, even if some of their methods were shaped by tradition.

But there came a time when I felt that quiet stirring inside— the kind you can't quite explain. Something felt missing. I couldn't shake the sense that there was *more*. And it wasn't condemnation. It wasn't fear. It was a whisper, a gentle nudge from Holy Spirit saying, "There's truth you haven't grasped yet. Come closer."

I thank Father for that inner witness. I thank Him that when I finally cried out, He didn't ignore me. He began to guide me, step by step. He started breaking down what I had built up—structures of performance, approval-seeking, and striving—and He began rebuilding me on the foundation of Christ by grace and relationship with Him.

I know many people have experienced deep hurt within the church. There are situations where leaders have misused their influence, causing wounds that take time and God's healing to mend. I never want to minimize that pain. But it's also true that pastors are human too. They carry burdens we don't always see and often bear the weight of expectations they never asked for. Sometimes, when life doesn't go the way we hoped, we place blame on spiritual leaders instead of reflecting on whether we sought God for ourselves. There were times when I didn't ask the hard questions or search the Scriptures like I should have. I simply accepted what I heard, and when things didn't turn out right, I felt frustrated—not realizing my own responsibility in the journey. Many good pastors have been left to take the fall when people leave ministries over misunderstandings or unmet expectations. At some point, we all must grow to seek God personally, to open His Word, and to let the Holy Spirit lead us into truth. By God's grace, that's where my journey began—and everything started to change.

Second Timothy 2:15 tells us, "Study to show yourself approved unto God, a workman that needeth not to be ashamed, rightly dividing the word of truth." At first glance, it might sound like Paul is saying we have to study to earn God's approval. But that's not the case. As believers, we are already approved through Christ— "accepted in the Beloved" (Ephesians 1:6). Our approval is based on His finished work, not our performance.

So, what does it mean to "study to show yourself approved"? It's about living as one who understands and honors the truth we've received. Paul was encouraging Timothy—from which we can learn— to be diligent, intentional, and accurate in how we handle the Word of God. This kind of study isn't about passing a spiritual test or gaining status. It's about being faithful stewards of truth, rightly dividing the Word so we're not led astray—or leading others astray.

Whether or not the Word is taught accurately from the pulpit, we are still called to pursue truth personally. You may have grown up tethered to tradition or shaped by a particular ministry, but spiritual growth requires personal pursuit. Yes, teachers are accountable for rightly dividing the Word, but that does not remove our responsibility to study, seek, and understand for ourselves.

When we study God's Word with the help of the Holy Spirit, we grow in discernment, depth, and relationship—not just knowledge. We become workers who need not be ashamed, because we know the truth and walk in it with confidence and grace.

So, this final conclusion is not with blame, but with ownership—and with deep gratitude. I thank God for His patience, His mercy, and His willingness to meet me exactly where I was, even though I had trapped myself.

Epilogue: Examine. Seek. Walk Free.

You've made it through these pages—but this is not the end. In many ways, it's only the beginning. This journey was never about gaining more head knowledge or collecting spiritual language. It was about helping you come face to face with the **real Jesus**—the One who sets captives free, renews the mind, and transforms the heart. And now, the question is simple:

What will you do with what you've read?
"Examine yourselves to see whether you are in the faith; test yourselves."
2 Corinthians 13:5 (NIV)

This isn't about doubt, it's about depth. It's an invitation to slow down, strip away every man-made layer, and get honest before Father.
- Are you walking in true freedom, or still trying to earn His love?
- Are you led by the Spirit, or driven by religious routine?
- Are you living in truth, or just carrying traditions?

You weren't made to live bound.

Examine Your Heart

Not in fear—but in faith. Ask the Holy Spirit to search you (Psalm 139:23–24). Be willing to let Him reveal where:
- You've settled for surface instead of depth
- You've obeyed tradition instead of truth
- You've kept Father at a distance instead of inviting Him into every part of you

There is no shame in honest repentance. There is only healing.

117

Seek Father for Yourself

Don't stop at this book. Go deeper. Take what stirred your heart and let it push you back to the **Word**, not just to another opinion or voice.

"You will seek me and find me when you seek me with all your heart."
Jeremiah 29:13 (NIV)

No preacher, teacher, or friend can seek Him for you. They can point the way, but **only you can choose to know Him for yourself**. He wants to speak to *you*. He wants to walk with *you*. He wants to reveal His love, His truth, His wisdom—to *you*.

Walk in the Freedom Christ Died to Give You

"It is for freedom that Christ has set us free. Stand firm, then, and do not let yourselves be burdened again by a yoke of slavery." — *Galatians 5:1 (NIV)*

You are not bound by the expectations of man. You are not chained to your past. You are not required to perform for Father's acceptance.

You are:
- **Loved**, unconditionally
- **Filled**, with the Spirit of Father
- **Equipped**, to walk in truth and power
- **Called**, to live a life that glorifies Him

Freedom is not found in spiritual appearances—it's found in surrender. In abiding. In choosing daily to believe what Father says over what others think.

This Is Your Call

Let this be your moment to say:

"I will no longer settle for a life of performance, passivity, or religious pressure. I will pursue Father—not through filters, but face to face. I will get into the Word for myself. I will walk by the Spirit. I will live in freedom, speak the truth in love, and finish my race in faith." Don't wait for someone else to lead. **You are the one Father is calling.**

So, rise up. Return to your first love. Let your life bear fruit. Let your heart burn again. And walk forward in the freedom that only Christ gives.

He's with you. He's in you. And He is more than enough.

Reader's Prayer of Commitment

Father,

I come before You with an open heart. I don't want to live by tradition, manmade rules, or performance anymore. I want You.

Search me. Show me anything in my life that doesn't reflect You. Help me to see rather than ignore, and repent for every time I've honored man's opinions above Your Word, and every time I've relied on manmade rules instead of Your truth.

Today, I choose to return to my first love—Jesus Christ.

I commit to seek You for myself—to open Your Word, listen to Your Spirit, and walk in truth no matter the cost.

I will not settle for shallow faith. I will not live bound by the fear of man. I will not chase platforms or approval. I will chase You.

Help me to bear fruit that honors You. Help me to keep a soft heart before You. Help my mind be renewed by truth. I pray that my days be marked by obedience, humility, and joy in Your presence.

Help me finish my race well. Not in my strength—but by Your Spirit.

Thank You for setting me free. Thank You for calling me higher. I belong to You.

In Jesus' name, Amen."

Declaration of Identity in Christ

I am not who the world says I am.

I am not who manmade rules told me I had to be.

I am who Father says I am.

I declare:

- **I am a new creation** in Christ.

  "Therefore, if anyone is in Christ, he is a new creation; the old has passed away, and see, the new has come!" — 2 Corinthians 5:17 (CSB)

- **I am deeply loved** by Father.

  "I have loved you with an everlasting love; I have drawn you with unfailing kindness." — Jeremiah 31:3 (NIV)

- **I am chosen, holy, and set apart.**

  "You are a chosen people, a royal priesthood, a holy nation, Father's special possession..." — 1 Peter 2:9 (NIV)

- **I am forgiven and free.**

  "So if the Son sets you free, you will be free indeed." — John 8:36 (NIV)

- **I am no longer a slave to sin.**

  "For sin shall no longer be your master, because you are not under the law, but under grace." — Romans 6:14 (NIV)

- **I have the Holy Spirit living in me.**

  "Do you not know that your bodies are temples of the Holy Spirit, who is in you...?" — 1 Corinthians 6:19 (NIV)

- **I have been given everything I need** for life and Fatherliness.

  "...His divine power has given us everything we need for a Fatherly life..." — 2 Peter 1:3 (NIV)

- **I am seated with Christ in heavenly places.**

  "Father raised us up with Christ and seated us with Him in the heavenly realms..." — Ephesians 2:6 (NIV)

- **I am Father's workmanship, created for purpose.**
  "For we are His workmanship, created in Christ Jesus to do good works…" — Ephesians 2:10 (NIV)
- **I am more than a conqueror through Christ.**
  "In all these things we are more than conquerors through Him who loved us." — Romans 8:37 (NIV)
- **I am His. I am secure. I am enough—because He is enough.**

Read this aloud regularly—especially in moments of doubt, fear, or temptation. Identity must be spoken, meditated on, and believed in the heart to transform a life.

Special Acknowledgment

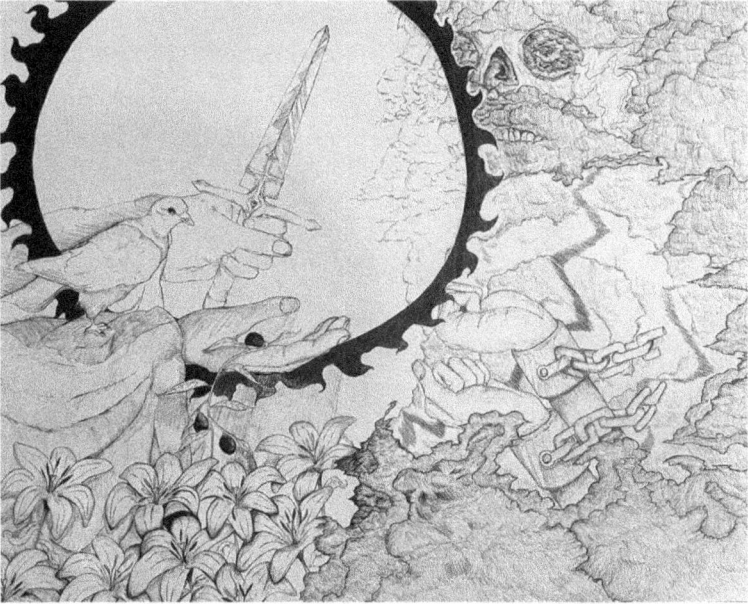

Throughout this book, I've honored Father, Son, and Holy Spirit. I've also acknowledged those in my Kingdom Family and community whose handprints have left a lasting impact on my life. But here, I want to give a special acknowledgment to my son, Marcel.

For years, I dreamed of writing a book, but I never quite pressed forward to do it. My pastor kept saying, "there are books in some of you." Then came the walks, the talks, and the deep conversations with my son. Little by little, those moments began to stir something in me. They sparked the courage and clarity I needed to finally write this book.

In 2024, Marcel drew the illustration featured above. It was done in ink and submitted to a contest—where he won first place. When I saw it, and then looked at the title of my book, I knew instantly: *this would inspire my cover*. His drawing visually captures the heart of everything this book stands for. I truly believe God birthed that image in him.

The light of God shining through Jesus, the breaking of chains, the dissipation of darkness—it all speaks of freedom. The dove represents the Holy Spirit, the sword stands for the Word of God, the olive branch symbolizes peace between God and man, and the lilies signify love.

Marcel, thank you for inspiring your mom in more ways than you know. I am so proud of the young man you are, and I love you deeply.

I'd like to also acknowledge my pastor. This acknowledgment does not imply Pastor Denise's agreement with every word written in this book. However, I would be remiss not to publicly thank her for her role in helping me steward this work more faithfully.

When I first shared with her that I had written a book, she asked to read it. I was both nervous and grateful—nervous because of the transparency of the content, and grateful because I knew she would read with spiritual sensitivity and a heart tuned to God. I prayed that the Lord would prepare my heart to receive any wisdom she might offer, and He answered that prayer.

In hindsight, I realize I almost released this book too soon. The time she spent with my unfinished manuscript turned out to be a divine delay. It gave me space to hear God more clearly, make necessary changes, and reexamine areas that could have unintentionally led someone in the wrong direction. As I suspected, her thoughtful notes confirmed what the Holy Spirit had already begun whispering to my heart.

Pastor Denise, thank you for your love, your honesty, and your obedience to speak truth with grace. True love corrects for the better, and this book is stronger, clearer, and more aligned with God's heart because of your input. I love you, and I am forever grateful for the way God worked through you.

Works Cited

The Holy Bible. Scripture quotations are taken from the following translations:

New King James Version (NKJV). Thomas Nelson, 1982.
New International Version (NIV). Biblica, 2011.
English Standard Version (ESV). Crossway, 2001.
King James Version (KJV). Public Domain.

Brother Lawrence. The Practice of the Presence of God. Translated by Marshall Davis, First Rate Publishers, 2016. Originally published 1692.

Dollar, Creflo A. Sermons and teachings aired on Changing Your World (television broadcast), 1990s–present.

Prince, Joseph. Destined to Reign: The Secret to Effortless Success, Wholeness and Victorious Living. Harrison House, 2007.

Prince, Joseph. The Power of Right Believing: 7 Keys to Freedom from Fear, Guilt, and Addiction. Faith Words, 2013.

Prince, Joseph. Unmerited Favor: Your Supernatural Advantage for a Successful Life. Harrison House, 2009.

"Relationship." Oxford English Dictionary, Oxford University Press, https://www.oed.com/. Accessed 9 July 2025.

Wommack, Andrew. Various teachings and books including Spirit, Soul & Body, Grace: The Power of the Gospel, and You've Already Got It!. Andrew Wommack Ministries, various years of publication.

Latonya Sterling

COMING SOON

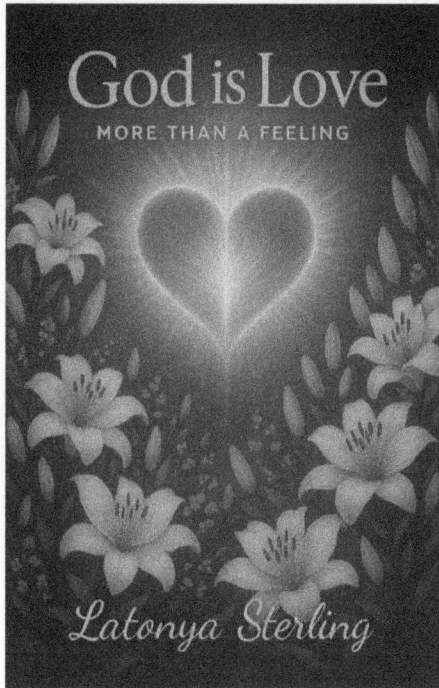

God is Love is not just a statement—it's a truth that transforms how we live, love, and see ourselves. This book explores what it truly means to experience God's love beyond religious performance, and how understanding His love impacts every area of our lives.

www.ingramcontent.com/pod-product-compliance
Lightning Source LLC
LaVergne TN
LVHW011206080426
835508LV00007B/623

*9 7 9 8 2 1 8 7 3 6 7 9 8 *